D1739514

CHURCHES IN ISTANBUL

Edith Oyhon was born in New York in 1923. She studied pharmaceutical sciences at the University of Pennsylvania. Oyhon has been living in Istanbul since 1952.

Bente Etingü was born in Oslo in 1946. She graduated from Stabekk Gymnasium in 1967 and studied history at Oslo University. She lives in Istanbul.

EDITH OYHON
and
BENTE ETİNGÜ

CHURCHES IN ISTANBUL

İSTANBUL

Yapı Kredi Publications
Art - 55

Churches In Istanbul
Photographs: Taner Dortunç

Editor: Ahu Antmen

Graphic Design: Nahide Dikel
Print: Altan Matbaacılık Ltd. Şti.

1. print: İstanbul, June 1999
ISBN 975-08-0026-5

Yapı Kredi Kültür Sanat Yayıncılık Ticaret ve Sanayi A.Ş.
Yapı Kredi Plaza E Blok Manolya Sokak 1. Levent 80620 İstanbul
Telefon: (0 212) 280 65 55 (pbx) Faks: (0 212) 279 59 64
http://www.ykykultur.com.tr
http://www.shop.superonline.com/yky
e-posta: ykkultur@ykykultur.com.tr

Contents

Preface

The Turkish Republic established in 1923 was founded as a secular state thanks to the wisdom and foresight of Mustafa Kemal Atatürk, its first president and founder of the republic.

Although the majority of the population in Turkey is Muslim, numerous non-Muslim communities live in the country. Though some of the members of the various groups have left the country, the remaining minorities still have their places of worship. Many have a long, historical past and Turkey is truly a gold-mine of information for comparative theology.

A variety of historical books on Istanbul are available in many languages. They may kindle an interest in the city that was once "The Rome of the East" and supplement the information of this book. It is certainly worth having one because you may be pleasantly surprised to discover new spots when roaming about.

It is not just historical buildings and their architecture that attract one's attention but also all the helpful people you meet along the way, the numerous children shouting "Hello" to visitors and foreign-looking tourists.

Over the centuries Istanbul has survived numerous fires, earthquakes and internal upheavals so it has lost some of its ancient charm and colour. Do not get discouraged by some of the dilapidated areas you may come across – neglected buildings, abandoned houses or just piles of stones. Use your imagination and you may visualize the history behind them all.

In no way is this book intended to be a study of the various Christian groups, churches and sites found in the city and its surroundings. It is meant to serve as a guide to most of the religious sites of the city.

Acknowledgements

We would like to thank the various individuals whom we met along the way, and kindly answered our questions, and helped in finding the many addresses. We give special thanks to the various Church Leaders in Istanbul who not only encouraged us but also contributed information about their churches. Special thanks go to Dorothy Irmak, Martha Millet for their help in correcting the material, and to Sibel Esen for typing the manuscript and to Taner Dortunç for his photography, not to mention the encouragement we got from our families and friends.

A Brief History of the City up to 1453

"The city of the living past, not the dead present."
Van Millingen

During the last three thousand years Istanbul has known three civilizations and has had several names including New Rome, Constantinople, Byzantium and Queen of Cities.

As far back as the 7th century B.C. a group of Greeks from the city of Megara, founded the city. Before leaving Megara, their leader, Byzas, a navigator, consulted an oracle who told him to make their new settlement "opposite the city of the blind".

When they arrived at the peninsula where the Marmara Sea merges with the Bosphorus they were attracted by its beauty. They quickly noticed the site's geographical advantages of being surrounded by water on three sides. Across the narrow strip of sea, the Bosphorus, that separated Europe from Asia they saw Chalcedon (Kadıköy) on the Asiatic side and realized that its position was not nearly as promising from either a commercial or a defensive point of view as their chosen spot. Then they understood the meaning of the oracle's words. Chalcedon was to be recognized as "the city of the blind" since its inhabitants had not observed the much more strategic spot located opposite them. Byzas and his followers chose to name their settlement Byzantium.[1]

To the north of Byzantium was an inlet from the sea. It formed a splendid natural harbor, the Golden Horn. Ships could pass through the Bosphorus, enter the Black Sea and sail northwestward to parts serving central Europe. They could also sail eastwards to parts which handled Caucasian trade. From there the routes connected to countries like India and China. Overland routes from Western Europe to Byzantium could easily be reached. From there travelers had only to cross the narrow Bosphorus to continue to either Asia or even Africa. Because of its favourable location, Byzantium came to play an important role in Greek history. It was often referred to during the wars with the Persians.

After the Peloponnesian wars of 196 A.D. it remained a member city of the Roman Empire until 324 A.D. The old Byzantium at that period of time covered only the area which today extends around "Saray Burnu" and Topkapı. It was enlarged and rebuilt along Roman style.

At the beginning of the 4th century A.D. after Emperor Diocletian's[2] retirement in 305, his two co-emperors fought one another bitterly around Chrysopolis (Üsküdar) for the control of the empire. The struggle was won by Constantine, Emperor of the West who in 324 defeated Licinius, Emperor of the East. The same year Byzantium surrendered to Constantine. He was now the sole ruler of the Roman Empire, naming his new capital Constantinople. When he arrived at the city, the Virgin Mary became its patron saint and it was called "the well-guarded city of God."

The project of building pagan Byzantium into Christian Constantinople took four years and on the 11th of May 330 A.D. Constantine dedicated the city of New Rome. This date is still celebrated within the Orthodox Church. As for

---

1   The name of the original city founded by th Megarians under Byzas, later to be named Constantinople. Byzantine is used to describe many forms of art that developed from the 4th century to the city's fall in 1453.
2   A pagan Roman Emperor (284 - 305)

Constantine, he was officially baptized shortly before his death. The Byzantine Empire is said to have come into being at this time and to have ended when that same city fell to the Ottoman Turks in 1453.

During these eleven centuries Byzantium underwent great changes. Its history can be divided into at least three major periods - the Early, the Middle and the Late. The Early period extended to about the middle of the 7th century with the rise of Islam and the permanent settlement of the Muslim Arabs along the eastern and southern shores of the Mediterranean. The Middle period lasted up to the occupation of Asia Minor by the Ottoman Turks in 1071 or as other sources claim, to the capture of Constantinople by the Crusaders in 1204.

The Late period is from either one of these dates to the fall of Constantinople in 1453.

Of the three periods, the Early is the most important due to great emperors like Constantine, the founder of the city who gave Byzantium its spiritual focus. It was the first city to base its existence on Christian principles. The Byzantines were among the first to confer the title "Great" on their first emperor, a verdict which later historians have confirmed. Theodosius (378-395) who proclaimed Christianity as the official religion, constructed the giant landwalls of the city which can still be seen today. He enlarged his empire and founded and rebuilt cities, monasteries and churches.

With Justinian the Great (527-565) big changes took place in art and religious thought. He had Hagia Sophia erected and a new Byzantine culture was rapidly created. These changes, rather than his success in uniting the empire, were to make Justinian famous. His codification of the Roman law was to be more permanent.

The middle period at the end of the 6th century of Justinian's empire was threatened by the peoples of the north. The Danube frontiers were attacked by the Avars, a Central Asian people. They were resisted by Justinian's successors.

But then came new waves of invaders such as the Slavs. Order within the government began to collapse. As new attacks were initiated from the north, other attacks were matched from the east. The Persians staged their most successful invasion ever. They crossed the entire length of Anatolia and seized Byzantine provinces as for away as Egypt. Emperor Heraclius (610-641) was able to expel the Persians by 628 A.D. This effort proved to be most exhausting to both the Romans and Persians. As a result they were unable to stop the new enemy, the Arab armies.

They were sweeping out of the desert under the banner of Islam. In 654 A.D. the Arab armies occupied Anatolia, taking Ankara and other cities. Two attacks were made on Constantinople. The city walls were impregnable and the seiges were repulsed. Within the 300 years that followed the Byzantine state had numerous squirmishes in trying to recover some of their lost ground.

The Byzantines did not seem to realize that the Seljuks, a Turkish tribe from Middle Asia, were steadily marching westward. After having overrun the Arab lands from Egypt to Baghdad they were riding north towards Byzantium as far as Cappadocia.

1071 was a bad year for the Byzantines. At the Battle of Malazgirt[1], north of Lake Van, Seljuk horsemen under the leadership of Alparslan defeated the Byzantine army and Anatolia lay open to Turks who promptly began their conquest of the country. At times it seemed as though the Byzantines were winning and the Turks were losing. But the Byzantines were doomed to fail. The Crusaders in 1204 on route to Jerusalem sacked the city of its treasures and established a Latin kingdom which lasted till 1261. The once powerful empire was greatly reduced and its citizens became more dependent on the rising power of the Ottoman Turks whose realms slowly surrounded those of Byzantium.

---

1   The city in eastern Turkey where the Selçuk Turks defeated the Byzantines.

In 1453 Byzantium disappeared forever and within days the city was renamed "Islamboul", the city of Islam or as other sources claim "Istanbul" from the Greek "eis ten polin" meaning "to the city". Throughout these struggles, Byzantium was preeminently a city of churches.

The Byzantines set up a sanctuary in every spot that was beautiful and wherever worshippers would come. Various references claim there were 392, 428, or 463 churches: 24 were dedicated to some attribute of the Diety, 64 to the Holy Virgin, 22 to the Archangels, 18 to St. John the Baptist, 9 to prophets, 35 to apostles, 155 to other saints and martyrs and 95 connected to monasteries.

The Byzantine churches of today are but shadows of what they were. Many are no longer in existence. Some are in ruins, others are museums, some were turned into mosques, while only one is still an active church. One must keep in mind that their cornerstones were laid long before America was discovered, before the Crusaders poured in from Europe and before the Prophet Mohammed was even born.

Time and again one is left wondering how various monuments have survived at all. Many a quarried stone or chiselled marble may be the threshhold of some cafe, or tottering garden wall, whereas once it was part of a holy edifice.

Not only wars, at least 60 fires, numerous earthquakes, iconoclastic[1] controversies, the Latin conquest, but also the needs of habitation for each succeeding generation have played their part in changing the face of the city.

---

1 Icons are sacred images that are venerated in religious ceremonies by the Orthodox and Eastern Rites churches. Up to the 6-7th centuries A.D. icons were not greatly venerated but in time the people wanted something visible on which to focus their prayers. Rules were even laid down as to how the icons were to be made. With the Arab invation of the empire in 717 A.D., doubt arose about the prayers offered to the icons. It was against a mixture of superstitions that the emperor Leo III (717 - 741) saw that it was his duty to guide his people out of the error of their ways. Between 726 and 843 the iconoclastic movement outlawed the veneration of icons and carried out a massive destruction of icons, images and statues in churches and monasteries. This resulted in a very serious political-religious controversy of wholesale image breakage and a fanatical persecution of the iconodules, the image worshippers during the 8 - 9th centuries. Veneration was restored at the Council of Nicea in 787 A.D. only to be banned again in 815. The empress Theodora again restored them in 843.

Christianity and the Division of the Eastern and Western Churches

Much history has emitted from the Middle East and southern Turkey, especially the history of Christianity. No matter where we step in these places, we are bound to find something that recalls the past of this religion that sprang up in Israel and took root in Antioch (Antakya). The latter located in southeastern Turkey is one of the most important biblical sites of the New Testament. It was during the peak of the Roman Empire in the 1st century A.D. that an aspect of Judaism called Christianity began to spread through Asia Minor, North Africa, Greece and the surrounding territories.

By 40 A.D. this new religion had established itself as a movement throughout Palestine with Jerusalem as its center. Here its followers were known as the Nazarenes after the birthplace of Jesus. In Antioch a second center was becoming active. Here the group was called Christians, men of Christ (Christianoi). Some texts say that this term was used to describe a group attached to "Christoso", a Greek translation of the Hebrew term, Messiah, which meant the Anointed and later the Deliverer.

Through the fervent missionary work of Paul of Tarsus this new religion found its driving force. Some have referred to him as a religious genius and the second founder of Christianity. After Christ's death the Western church was established by the apostle Peter, "the Rock". He became the first Bishop[1] of Rome and was later recognized as the most important Christian figure.

Though the new religion was accepted and to some extent tolerated by the Romans there was a lot of persecution and the Christians were never secure. The worst persecution under the Emperor Diocletian[2] was at the beginning of the 4th century. Christianity however became the official religion of the Byzantine Empire with an edict of Theodosius I in 380 A.D. and this helped in its establishment.

The bishops of the East had started to split among themselves on various doctrinal controversies as far back as the first centuries of the church. No bishop had the authority to speak for all the Eastern churches. The West was relatively free of these rifts and so the Bishop of Rome was their unchallenged spokesman. At the beginning there existed a uniformity in belief and practice but in time contrasting interpretations of faith developed. In spite of these problems, Christianity was slowly transformed from a Middle Eastern religion to a European one.

After Constantine had established Constantinople as the new capital of the Eastern Roman Empire, the rift between the Eastern and Western Christians based on political, geographical and theological differences started to widen. Between 325 and 1445 there were 17 General Ecumenical[3] Councils of the Church.

The first four were the Councils of Nicea, Constantinople, Ephesus and Chalcedon which dealt with the Christological problems involved in the doctrine of the incarnati-

---

1 St. Peter wes the first Bishop of Rome because Rome was among the first Christian centers and he had primacy among the apostles as designated by Christ. Up to the 4-5th centuries any bishop was called "Pope". The restriction of the word "Pope" to the Bishop of Rome occurred gradually over a period of time. It did not come about completely until after the 5th century A.D.
2 A pagan Roman Emperor (284-305)
3 Universal church, of or representing the whole Christian world.

on. The fifth and sixth ones, Constantinople II and III further defined the theology of Chalcedon. The seventh, Nicaea II upheld the use of images in divine worship in opposition to the iconoclasts.

These seven councils are recognized by the Eastern Orthodox Church. The Roman Catholics acknowledge ten more councils mainly concerned with matters of discipline.

The struggles for power in the leadership of Christianity by either the Greek Orthodox Church or the Church of Rome, led to the seperation of the churches. There were also differences of rituals such as baptisim of children by immersion, giving the communicants both wine, bread and the use of icons and the dates for celebrating Easter. At the beginning of Christianity the priests could be married. Then in time the Orthodox further demanded celibacy for their bishops but the priests and deacons were allowed to marry before ordination.

The liturgical language was Greek and not Latin and this also caused problems between the groups.

The Roman church permitted religious statues in their worship. They gave their communicants only bread as communion at mass. By the end of the 4th century the tradition of celibacy for priests, deacons and bishops was established. Until the middle of the 20th century the liturgical language of the church was Latin.

In 1054 Pope Leo IX sent delegates to excommunicate the Patriarch of Constantinople because he had closed the Latin churches. This was really the climax of the conflicts that existed at the time. All hope of unity between the two rites was completely lost after the pillage and vandalism of the city by the Crusaders in 1204.

The term Orthodox was then used to identify:

a) The churches not united with Rome

b) The Christian churches of countries that were in communion or doctrinal agreement with the Patriarch of Constantinople

c) The churches that were evangelized by the Byzantine Empire

The original language was Greek therefore it was named the Greek Orthodox Church. As other Orthodox churches were established, they adopted their national languages in their liturgies, the Bulgarian Orthodox using Slavonic, the Armenian Orthodox their Armenian tongue etc.

The Orthodox churches that are found in Istanbul are the Greek, Russian, Bulgarian, Armenian (Gregorian), Syrian (Süryani) and Turkish.

Byzantine Churches
That Are Now in Ruins

St. Polyeuktos

Location: Saraçhane on Atatürk Blvd. in the park across the street from the Municipal Building.

This church was built between 524-527 A.D. for a princess, Anicia Juliana and was one of the earliest sanctuaries erected during the reign of Emperor Justinian. It was an enormous building some 52 m. on one side and is said to have been the second largest church in Constantinople after Hagia Sophia. The ruins were found in the mid-1960's during the excavations for the Atatürk Blvd. underpass. The excavation was supervised by Martin Harrison for Dumbarton Oaks, an archeological society from Boston. The fragments of the columns, capitals and other structural pieces by which the building was identified are quite impressive and can be seen in the park.

St. John of Studion
Imrahor Camii

Location: Samatya

This interesting church together with the Monastery of St. John the Baptist was founded in 463 A.D. by the patrician, Studius. The monastery was inhabited by a strange com-

St. John of
Studion

munity of monks-the Sleepless Monks-(Akoimati, Acoeme-
ti, Akoemetae, Acemetes) so called because they were divided into three groups, Greek, Latin and Syrian which rela-
yed one another, day and night to give unceasing praise to
God around the clock and the calendar. It was one of the richest monasteries in Byzantium and housed a thousand
monks. One of its greatest abbots was Theodosius Studita
(759-826) who had been greatly influenced by St. Basil. A
portrait of the latter can be seen in the frescoes in the parecclesion of the Kariye Museum.

There was an intense religious life at the Studion. The
mortifications were harsh, the discipline severe, the fasts ri-
gurous and the spirit of poverty so extreme that each week
the monk's clothing was placed in a heap from which each
monk took the first garment that came to hand. Not only
did they have to pray but were obliged to study and pass
their time in copying historical works, gospels and calenders

with marginal illustrations. It was one of the great centers for preserving and copying ancient scripts which were eventually carried away to Europe by Byzantine scholars during the Western Renaissance of the 14-15th centuries. The church and monastery remained a center of spiritual and intellectual learning up to the time of the conquest of Constantinople in 1453. The University of Constantinople was located here during the first half of the 15th century During the Latin Occupation (1204-1261) the church was pillaged and ruined by the Crusaders. Some capitals from this church were transported to the Church of the Wisdom of God in Lower Kingswood, Surrey England. The Emperor Michael Palaiologos (1261-1282) had the church repaired and the floor decorated with magnificent mosaics, some being still visible.

Imperial visits were paid annually on Aug. 29th commemorating the martyrdom of St. John the Baptist. On that occasion the emperor came from the Great Palace by sea and landed in state at the pier of the nearby gate, Narlı Kapı, where he was received by the abbot and the monks. The most important act that he performed during the religious service was to incense the remains of the skull of St. John the Baptist that was enshrined in the church. Today it can be found in the Topkapı Museum.

There had been controversies between the monks and ruling family because of their behavior. The Studites were very influential in church matters.

The relics preserved in the church drew devout pilgrims from near and far. Many Russians visited this church and even entered the Order of the Studites to live and die there. A humble tombstone of one of these Russian monks was built in the base of a wall behind the apse. It carried the inscription "In the month of September of the year 1387, fell asleep the servant of God, Dionysius, a Russian, on the sixth day."

The Studion was finally turned into a mosque during

the reign of Sultan Bayezid II (1481-1512). The Sultan had an Ilyas Bey in his service who was "The Master of the Horses"- the Imrahor. The mosque was so named after him. It was abandoned after an earthquake brought down most of it in 1894. The Russian Archeological Institute did some research there and certain pieces were placed in the Museum of Antiquities. The mosque is offically under the administration of the Hagia Sophia Foundation. South of the church there is a cistern having Corinthian capitals but it is in ruins due to a fire in 1782.

St. Mary Chalkoprateia

Location: Alemdar Sok. across the walls of Topkapı Palace near the Zeynep Sultan Camii, Sultan Ahmet

This church was one of the most famous churches in Constantinople. Its origin is unclear. According to Justinian Verine it was built by the wife of Leo I (457-474) Theodosios the Lector said that Pulcheria, sister of Theodosius II (408-450) founded it by converting a synagogue of the Chalkoprateia (the copper-makers) that had been there. After the Nika[1] Revolt of 532 when Hagia Sophia had been destroyed, it served as the Patriarchal Cathedral for a time. The church seems to have been a basilica[2]. Today only scattered ruins remain of the once famous church. When one looks at the ruins, a super imagination is helpful.

Martyrium of Hagia Euphemia of Chalcedon

Location: Sultanahmet

Nothing but a few ruins survive today. The relics of this martyr who died in about 307. A.D. are to be found in the Greek Patriarchate. She was one of the victims of the Dioc-

---

1 There were two parties in Constantinople, one being the "Blues" a party of the aristocracy and strict orthodoxy. The other was the "Greens" a party of the lower classes and questionable orthodoxy. These two factions would invade each others quarters, burn down houses, and cause general disorder.

2 A building, especially a church whose central area is separated from the sides aisles by rows of columns with an apse at one end.

letian persecutions. The original building is said to have been built as a palace for a nobleman named Antiochus and later converted to a church dedicated to this saint. During excavations in Sultanahmet in 1939 this church was unearthed. Most of the frescoes have been destroyed.

St. Saviour Philanthropos

Location: Past the lighthouse that faces the Asiatic coast on the Marmara Sea, along the sea-walls, on the coast road going up from Sirkeci.

This is another ruined church that can tax one's imagination. About half a km. up the road from the lighthouse one comes to the "Pearl Pavilion" (İncili Köşk), built at the end of the 16th century by Murat III (1574-1595). A little further up the facade of the church can be seen. Only blocked up niches, windows, doors and huge arch are visible. It was built by Alexios I Komnenos (1081-1118). There are believed to be many substructures of ancient churches in this area which is presently a military zone.

Byzantine Churches
That Are Now Museums

St. Saviour in Chora
Kariye Müzesi

Location: Edirnekapı

The original sanctuary is said to have existed on this site prior to 413 A.D. and restored as a basilica by Justinian (527-565). There had also been a convent that was ruined during the iconoclastic persecutions of Constantine V Kopronymos (741-775).

However the church was again restored by Mary Doukas, a niece of Isaac Komnenos (1057-1059). When the Latins evacuated Constantinople, the building was again in ruins to be restored this time by Theodore Metochites, the treasurer in the reign of Andronikos II Palaiologos (1282-1328). His mosaic portrait can be seen over the door looking from the inner narthex[1] into the nave. His restotation was a labour of love, but one that left him a penniless, miserable monk. He was buried in the parecclesion, a side chapel of the church.

Not until the 15th century was it converted to a mosque by Bayezid II's vezir[2], Atik Ali Paşa when all the frescoes

---

1 The narthex is the long narrow porch, usually archaded at the entrance of a church. Occasionally an additional vestibule exists within the church proper. Then the inner vestibule is the narthex and the outer one is the exonarthex.

2 An adviser or minister.

St. Saviour in Chora, inner narthex dome.

and mosaics were painted and plastered over. Up to 1860 they were unknown to scholars until a Greek architect, Pelopidas Kouppas, uncovered them. After the Turkish republic was established the building was repaired and restored by Paul A. Underwood of the American Byzantine Institute in the 1950s and 1960s and later was opened as a museum.

Much can be written about the art and architecture of the church but it is more practical to obtain one of the numerous books that are available. The Byzantine art viewed here dates back at least a hundred years before the Rennaisance. Though much art was destroyed during the iconoclastic struggle, it was to be reborn in the 9th century. A visit to this museum should not be rushed. Leave yourself plenty of time to study some of the most beautiful mosaics and frescoes in the world such as the mosaics depicting the story of the life of the Virgin Mary. The parecclesion portrays the themes of the resurrection in beautiful frescoes.

While there, sit in one of the tea-gardens, take a well deserved rest and gaze at the pleasant and colourful neighbourhood that has been restored.

St. Saviour in Chora

The Church of St. Irene, Church of Divine Peace
Aya Irini

Location: Sultanahmet, at the entrance to Topkapı Palace

This churh was built on the site of a pagan temple to Aphrodite. When Constantine the Great took over the city in 324 A.D. he enlarged and dedicated it to "Peace" in honour of the rest and quiet which had settled upon the Roman world when all his rivals had vanished after 18 years of civil war. It was one of the Christian sanctuaries of Byzantium and the cathedral of the city until 360 A.D. when the first Hagia Sophia was completed. It did not lose its importance even then. On the contrary both churches had a common courtyard, were served by the same clergy and formed what was known as the "Mega Ekklesia", the Great Church.

During the reign of Theodosius I the Constantinople I Ecumenical Council on the Divinity of the Holy Spirit met here in 381 A.D. Together with Hagia Sophia it was damaged as a result of a fire in 532 A.D. and had to be rebuilt by Justinian. Again it was destroyed by an earthquake, to be restored and enlarged by Leo the Isurian. During the iconoclastic period all the mosaics and frescoes were destroyed and replaced by simple crosses, one of which can still be seen in the semi-dome of the apse, as a reminder of this period.

After the conquest of Constantinople[1] in 1453 the church was neither converted into a mosque nor destroyed. It was used as an arsenal until the reign of Ahmet III (1704-30) and established as a museum by Fethi Ahmet Paşa during the reign of Abdulmecit (1839-67). In 1875 the collection was moved to the Archeological Museum and the building was converted to a military museum. During the Second World War (1939) the arms displayed were sent to Niğde in Anatolia for safe keeping. The holes that are seen in the walls were used to display military standards.

The Church of
St. Irene

1   The name of the city before the Turkish conquest of 1453 later to be called Istanbul.

Today it is one of the most popular cultural buildings of Istanbul being used for various art displays, exhibitions and concerts. When the Istanbul Foundation for Culture and Art was founded it was suggested that this building be used for some of its music programs but it was uncertain whether such an ancient structure could withstand the musical vibrations. So the "Mehter Band", which had first been established as a ceremonial marching military band of the Ottoman times was brought in to perform. After the band had played a number of vibrant and boisterous pieces no damage to the building resulted. This was certainly a very practical way to test the safety of the building.

Every summer since 1972 during the Istanbul Music Festival choirs, ensembles, quartets, many Turkish and foreign artists including Yehudi Menuhin, David Oistrakh have performed here. It is said that when Menuhin was asked to play at the first festival one of his conditions was to play at Aya Irini because of the wonderful acoustics. In October 1987 there was a program performed by the Augsburger Domsingknaben Choir commemorating the 1200th anniversary of the Council of Nicaea (İznik). If you are here during the music festival which is usually held from mid-June to the end of July, try to find a ticket for one of the performances, though it may be difficult to do so. It would be a memorable occasion.

Take the time to sit on the outside walls of the church, look down and see the various marble stones and columns. They are from the Temple of Aphrodite but there has not been time to label and arrange them.

Haghia Sophia, Church of the Divine Wisdom
Aya Sofya Müzesi

Location: Sultanahmet

As Van Milligen put it, "the influence of Hagia Sophia upon the history of art has been greater than any other building" and it is still considered to be an unparalelled architectural monument. The present structure is the third church to have been built on the site and dedicated to "Holy Wisdom". The first church was opened on May 12, 360 A.D. and together with Aya Irini was known as the Mega Ekklesia. On June 20, 404 it was burned in a rebellion that took place because Bishop John Chrysostom[1] had been exiled. It was rebuilt by Theodosius II and reopened for worship on Oct 8, 415. Again it was entirely burned down during the Nika rebellion on the night of Jan 13, 532.

Justinian then decided to build a new church, making it the most magnificent of all existing churches. He personally laid the first foundation stone of the church for he wanted to create a church such as, according to one historian, "had never existed since the time of Adam and such as will never be equalled". The foremost architects and engineers of the time, Anthemios of Tralles and Isidore of Miletus planned and built the church. Prokopios, the historian, added that "it was evident that God protected Justinian since he had prepared for him the most capable men to carry out his project". The emperor personally supervised the building. On its inauguration of Dec. 26, 537 he was welcomed by the Patriarch Menas. Upon entering the church he was so inspired by the glory and magnificence of the structure that he raised his hands and cried "Thanks be to God who made me worthy to surpass even thee, O Solomon".

---

1 (347-407), born in Antioch, baptized in 370 A.D. a brilliant Christian orator, a doctor of the East who gave the scriptures their literal and grammatical sense. Processional church music and singing were introduced by him to keep the masses coming to church. The Greek and Latin churches both revere him as a Father of the church. The Greek Orthodox Church celebrates his feast on Nov. 13 and the Latin church on Jan. 27.

*The Hagia
Sophia*

The church served as a religious ceremonial center for the imperial family and for daily and holy-day services for the congregation. Its entrance was from the narthex through nine doors. The large magnificent central door, the imperial gate, was reserved for the ceremonial entrance of the Emperor and the Patriarch.

Besides all the historical facts that have been recorded about the church there are many legends too. One is that the imperial door was made from wood that came from Noah's Ark. Travellers prayed before the door before embarking on a voyage.

The central dom is 55.6 m from the floor and it is about 33 m in diameter. Standing below it enhances one's appreciation of dimensions.

Women used the upper galleries for worship. To reach them one has to climb a ramp. Nobility did not climb stairs so this walk was built for the Empress Theodora and her royal cortege.

Over the 1400 years of its existence it has suffered much damage. One of the important reconstructions by the Armenian architect, Titidate, was made during the reign of Basil I (867-86). Part of the dome came down once more during an earthquake in 986 A.D. The Crusaders looted the church during the Latin occupation and sent many of its precious objects and relics to Europe. On May 29, 1453 the day of the Turkish conquest much of the city populace took refuge in the church. When Mehmet II, the Conqueror, entered the church on foot, he and his retinue said prayers according to the practices of Islam and it was dedicated as a mosque.

The minarets were added later at different periods. Many changes were made in the conversion from church to mosque. Since pictorial representations are traditionally not permitted in Islam, many mosaics were concealed under the plaster over the years.

When the Fossati brothers, Swiss-Italian architects were commissioned by Sultan Abdulmecid to repair the mosque in 1845, it is certain that they also plastered over many mosaics. These are the same architects who rebuilt the Dominican church of SS. Peter and Paul in Galata.

In 1932 the Ministry of Education upon order from Atatürk gave Prof. Thomas Whittemore, founder of the Byzantine Institute of America, permission to uncover and clean the mosaics. After his death in June 1949 the work was carried on for the Institute by Prof. Paul A. Underwood. Hagia Sophia had served 916 years as a basilica, 477 years as a mosque and finally since 1932 as a museum. It is among the most important Byzantine works that has survived to this day.

A Byzantine Church
That Is Part Museum and a Mosque

Church of Hagia Maria Pammakaristos,
Fethiye Camii

Location: Draman, Fethiye Caddesi

This was a church of a convent whose founder and date of foundation are not exactly known. One source states that it was built by John Komnenos and his wife Anna in the 12th century. It was completely restored between 1292-94 by Michael Glabas who is wrongly considered to be the founder. He was the nephew by marriage of Michael Palaiologos. His widow, Maria erected a chapel the parekklesion[1] in 1315 in his memory. On the exterior wall of the chapel there is the following Greek inscription:

"Oh, my husband, my light, the breath of my life. I salute thee. Take this from thy wife. As a lion vigilant in battle, death has found thee rather than peaceful seclusion in thy lair. But I have built for thee this house of stone that the army in finding thee, trouble thee not".

After the conquest in 1453, the Patriarch Gennadius[2] was given the Church of the Holy Apostles[3] as a patriarcha-

1 A side chapel.
2 In 1148 he was a monk at the Pantokrator. In 1453 Mehmet the Conqueror made him the Patriarch of Constantinople.
3 A church that existed where the present Fatih Mosque stands. It was named after the 12 disciples of Christ - Peter, James, John, Andrew, Philip, Bartholomew, Matthew, Thomas, Simon, Thaddaeus, Judas and Judas the Iscariot.

te. He stayed there for only two years as the surrounding quarter was largely inhabited by the Ottoman Turks and he preferred the Church of Pammakaristos which was more in the midst of his flock. Sultan Fatih Mehmet sometimes visited him and had long religious discussions with him.

The church remained the Patriarchate until the reign of Murat III who occupied it in 1591 and renamed it the Fethiye Camii - The Mosque of Victory - in honour of the conquest of Georgia and Azerbaidjan. The Patriarchate was then transferred to the Church of St. Demetrius Kanabu and finally in 1601 to the present church of St. George in Fener.

One source claims that this building has the most beautiful Byzantine exterior. A wall inside separates the mosque and museum sections. The chapel is the museum and it is administerd by the Hagia Sophia Foundation. The mosaics of Christ and the Apostles richly decorate the chapel and are much to be admired. If you climb the staircase, you will come up to the level of the dome and get a closer view of the mosaics. The Byzantine Institute of Boston carried out the restorations in the museum.

A Byzantine Church That is Still Active as a Greek Orthodox Church

Mary of the Mongols - Maria Mouchliotissa, *Kanlı Kilise*

Location: At the top of Sancaktar Yokuşu, a steep street that goes up next to the Greek Patriarchate in Fener.

Feast day: Aug. 15

In 1285 this church became the property of Mary Palaiologina, a daughter of Michael VIII Palaiologos (1259-82). Early in his reign Michael entered into an alliance with Hulagu, the great Khan of the Mongols, Hulagu tended to favour the Christians because there were Nestorian Christians among the Mongols.

So in 1265 it was arranged between the two courts for Mary to wed Hulagu but on arrival at the Mongol court she found that he had died. She then married his son Abagu (Abaka) who was later assassinated by his brother Ahmet. Mary returned home to found a church and a convent dedicated to the Virgin of the Mongols so that souls wishing to live for God could find spiritual refuge there. She became a nun and spent her years of retirement in her convent.

At the request of Mehmet II's Greek architect, Christodoulos, the sultan issued an imperial decree allowing the Greek community ownership of this church.

There are still many religious treasures to be found here from the Byzantine period. Among them is a portative mosaic of "Theodokos Pammakaristos" - the all Joyous Mother of God. The Turks named the church "Kanlı Kilise", the Church of Blood for in the neighbouring street of Sancaktar Yokuşu - the Standard Bearers' Mount - fierce struggles took place on the day that the city was taken by the Turks.

Byzantine Churches That Were Converted to Mosques After 1453

St. Andrew in Krisei (Judgement)
Koca Mustafa Paşa Camii

Location: Kocamustafapaşa

There are various tales about the beginnings of this church. It is said to have been founded by the sister of Theodosius II (408-50) at the beginning of the 5th century and dedicated to St. Andrew the Apostle who according to tradition helped to form the first Christian community of Byzantium. Later it was rededicated to St. Andrew of Crete who was martyred during the reign of the iconoclast Constantine V Kopronymos (741-75). Basil I (867-86) restored it in the 9th century. In 1261 at the end of the Latin rule in Constantinople it was enlarged by Theodora, a niece of Michael VIII Palaiologos.

The church was converted to a mosque by the Grand Vezir Koca Mustafa Paşa in the reign of Selim I (1512-20) and named after him. According to a legend a chain hung for centuries from an old cypress tree in the courtyard. This chain was able to settle disputes miraculously.

Much of the original structure has changed. The interior was plastered, a portico was added along the north flank and the exterior was completely refinished in limestone. Some of the original columns with Byzantine capitals are still to be seen.

It is one of the more frequently visited Muslim religious shrines.

SS. Peter and Mark, Atik Mustafa Paşa Camii

Location: Up on the Golden Horn - Mustafa Paşa Bostanı Sok., Ayvansaray

There are still some controversies about the original name and the church's date of foundation. But it is said to have been built in 458 A.D. during the reign of Leo I by the patricians[1] Galbien and Candidus. It housed the holy tunic of the Virgin which had been brought from Jerusalem. The tunic was taken to St. Mary of Blachernai by order of Justinian and it was the palladium[2] of the city preserving the city from sicknesses and enemies. The present mosque does not date back to the 5th century. It was rebuilt at a later unknown date. Compared to many places in this category it looks clean both inside and outside, with a small, well-kept garden around the mosque.

Sergios and Bakchos, Church of Saints
Küçük Ayasofya Camii

Location: At the end of the Hippodrome behind the Sultan Ahmet mosque, at the bottom of Aksakal Sok. along the R.R. tracks.

This building is so named because of its supposed resemblance to Hagia Sophia in splendor and architectural style. It was originally dedicated to Sergios and Bakchos, two Christian officers in the Roman army of Maximus during the 4th century. Legend states that they were massacred by that tyrant for refusing to pay homage to Jupiter. They became the patron saints of the Byzantine army and the Christians in the Roman army.

---

1 Members of old Roman citizen families.
2 Anything regarded as an important safeguard.

A cult of Sergios was widespread and the nomads of the desert looked upon him as their special patron. His feast day is Oct. 8.

It seems that Justinian and his uncle Justin had been accused of plotting against the Emperor Anastasios I (491-518) and were condemned to a hasty execution. On the eve of their execution the Emperor saw Sergios and Bakchos in a dream. The saints' proved the prisoners' innocence and threatened Anastasios with the wrath of God unless they were restored to liberty and honour. Justinian remembered this heavenly intervention which had saved his life and on accession to the throne in 527, he consecrated his entire fortune to the erection of a church as a votive offering to the two saints.

Pope Vigilius (555) was invited to Constantinople by Theodora to settle a theological question. It was at a time when there were good relations between the Byzantine Empire, the Western Holy Roman Empire and the papacy. But Vigilius was anti-Justinian in his decisions and was excommunicated by the Patriarch Menas who was close to Justinian. The Pope sought sanctuary in this church.

The abbot of the church was the distinguished iconoclast Patriarch John VII. Whenever the papal legates or the Pope himself were in Constantinople they officiated at its altar. On the Tuesday of Easter week the Emperor and his court prayed here and he himself assisted in the liturgy. This sanctuary to which the court came with great pomp was one of the richest in the city.

During the Latin occupation it was ruined and then repaired by Michael VII. After the Ottoman Conquest it was converted to a mosque by Hüseyin Ağa, chief of the white Eunuchs. He fell out of favour and was beheaded and buried out-side the mosque.

Sergios and Backhos, Church of Saints

It has been recorded that during the Russian-Turkish war from 1877-79 hordes of Bulgarian Muslim refugees sought refuge within the garden walls of this mosque. On the southern side of the church between two small columns was the imperial entrance above which can be seen the clearcut monograms of Theodora and Justinian. In 1860 when the adjoining train tracks were laid, some of its foundation was destroyed but finally restored in 1937.

Much detailed literature is available about this building and its environs.

St. John the Baptist in Trullo (of the Dome),
Hirami[1] Ahmet Paşa Camii

Location: Draman, off Fethiye Cad. in the neighbourhood of Fethiye Camii.

Historians claim that the date of origin is unknown. Certain writers believe that the famous "Quinisextum[2] Council in Trullo" of 691-692 in the reign of Justinian II was held here.

After the conquest of 1453 the church was used as a chapel by some orthodox nuns who had been at Pammakaristos (Fethiye Camii) during the period when it was the patriarchal church and Gennadios had them transferred to this church. They lived here until 1586 when it was renamed and converted to a mosque.

This small building was partially restored a few years ago and whatever frescoes existed were destroyed. The building has lost its charm. The windows are covered with chicken-wire and the mosque seems squeezed in by the neighbourhood buildings.

St. Theodosia
Gül Camii

Location: Aya Kapı on the Golden Horn

St. Theodosia was probably the Church of St. Euphemia built by Basil I at the end of the 9th century and rededicated to St. Theodosia. When the iconoclastic Emperor Leo III the Isaurian (717-41) ordered the image of Christ surmounting the bronze door of the great Hagia Sophia to be taken down, a woman named Theodosia, attacked the scaffolding. The soldiers seized her and tragically killed her. At

---

1 A Janissery general. "Hirami" stands for either the place he was born or it is a nickname.

2 "Fifth-Sixth". Council of Trullo, 692 so called because it was considered complementary to the 5th and 6th councils. It set up regulations about celibacy, clerical maarriages, pagan celebrations on May Day or at the wine harvest as well as certain magical practices. It was the cause for some more alienation between the Eastern and Western churches.

the end of the iconoclastic oppression she was honoured as a martyr. The church played an important part in Byzantine history. Processions of relics took place twice a week and miraculous cures were attributed to them.

On May 28, 1453 the eve of the fall of Constantinople, Constantine went to church in preparation of the saint's feast day. When the Ottomans entered the city the next day they found the church full of roses and some claim that this may be the reason it was given its name of "Gül Camii" - the Mosque of the Roses. This legend is unlikely to be true for it did not become a mosque until more than 200 years later. Another belief is that the mosque was named after a Muslim saint "Gül Baba" who rebuilt it as a mosque. According to another reference the church stayed in the hands of the Greeks until the reign of Sultan Selim (1566-74) when it was taken from them and given to the Dominicans and renamed the Church of Sancta Rosario. The Dominicans kept the church until 1629, after which time it was converted to a storehouse for the Ottoman navy because it was near the great arsenal on the Golden Horn. During Süleyman II's reign it was converted to a mosque.

St. Nicholas, Convent of Manuel
Kefeli Camii or Mescidi[1]

Location: Draman, Draman Cad.

There are a few conflicting stories about this small Byzantine church which became Latin and later a mosque. Some say it was founded by a General Manuel who conquered the Saracens[2] in the reign of Theophilos (829-42). Others say that it was founded by another Manuel who was Theodora's uncle and regent of Michael III (842-67). Then Patriarch Photius had it reconstructed and the co-emperor Romanos I Lekapenos (914-44) restored it. The Emperor Michael VII Doukas (1071-78) called Parapinakes when he

1   A small mosque like a chapel
2   Muslims at the time of the Crusades.

was deposed in 1078 and became the Archbishop of Ephesus ended his days here.

In 1475 a general of Mehmet the Conqueror named Gedik Ahmet Paşa took the town of Kaffa in Crimea. Colonies of Armenians and Genoese who had been brought from Kaffa, were given the convent which was then served by the Dominicans from the church of SS. Peter and Paul in Galata. They named it St. Nicholas and the Latin creed was practiced there until 1630.

Murat IV (1623-40) converted it to a mosque. The Turks who had lived in Kaffa called the city "Kefe" and so their place of worship was named "Kefeli Camii."

Myrelaion-Oil of Myrrh,
Bodrum Camii

Location: Laleli, Sait Efendi Sok. just off Ordu Cad.

The origin and builder are much disputed but the common belief is that the church was built as part of the Monastery of Myrelaion.

In the middle of the 8th century Constantine Kopronymos V, the iconoclast (741-75) had the convent closed and so the nuns had to move. Romanus I Lekapenos (920-44) who was co-emperor with Constantine VII Porphyrogennetos, restored the church. Adjoining it was his palace of which some remains can still be seen near the rotunda. This rotunds was originally the reception hall of the palace but was later turned into a cistern.

Many fires ruined the church which was later converted to a mosque by Mesih Ali Paşa who was a governor of Egypt in the reign of Murat III (1572-95). In 1911 a fire destroyed the surrounding neighbourhood and the mosque was restored much later to be used as such in 1985. The church was built over a crypt where several emperors and their families were buried. This crypt can be entered by going through a shop on a side street next to the mosque therefore it was named "The Mosque with the Cellar".

St. Mary Diakonissa, Theotokos Kyriostissa, The Church of the Monastery of Akataleptos
Kalenderhane Camii

Location: Beyazıt, near the Aqueduct of Valens, not far from the dormitory of the Pharmacy school

From 1967-72 Prof. Lee Striker of the Dumbarton Oaks Society directed the archeological restoration of this building along with the Istanbul Technical University. Some scholars said that it was the church of St. Mary Diakonissa; others, of St. Akataleptos; but Striker identified the building as the church of Theotokos Kyriostissa from the second half of the 9th century.

During the 11th century many theological lectures were given here. In 1367 the Orthodox Synod[1] met in the church.

It had been rebuilt and restored many times during the Byzantine and Ottoman periods. One can find various marble structures and sculptured decorations in the building. Of interest are the frescoes that Striker found, especially the scenes from the life of St. Francis of Assisi painted only a few years after his death in 1226 during the latter part of the Latin occupation of Constantinople when Franciscan monks lived here. The frescoes were removed for safe-keeping but the place of storage has not been revealed.

After the Conquest of Constantinople in 1453 it became a tekke (lodge) for a Muslim order of dervishes of the Kalender order and so it was named the "Kalenderhane Camii".

---

1 An assembly of clergy discussing ecclessiastical affairs

Monastery of Constantine Lips

Monastery of Constantine Lips
Fenari Isa Camii

Location: Aksaray on Vatan Cad

Constantine Lips, a courtier of Leo the Wise and Constantine VII Porphyrogennetos dedicated the first church to the Immaculate Mother of God in 908. Over 350 years later in the reign of Michael VIII Palaiologos (1259-82) Theodora, his wife, reopened the monastery and added a new church that of St. John the Baptist. The monastery was said to have had 50 nuns and also a 15 bed hospital. Both Theodora, Michael VIII Pallaiologos' wife and Irene, the first wife of Andronikos II (1282-1328) were confined in the monastery. Adronikos II became a monk before he abdicated in 1328, dying in 1332.

The church was converted to a mosque during the reign of Bayezid II (1481-1512) by Alaeddin Ali bin Yusuf Fenari who was a military authority in command of Thrace.

The mosque suffered severe damage in a great fire in 1633 but was restored and its minaret and mihrab renewed in 1636. The mosque was the scene of the massacres of the Janissaries[1] in 1826. Although not completely damaged by fire in 1917, it was abandoned and in 1947 came under the administration of the Hagia Sophia Foundation later to be partially restored by the Byzantine Institute. From 1967 onward it has once more been used as a mosque.

St. Saviour Pantepoptes, Christ the All-Seeing
Eski İmaret Camii

Location: Fatih, Küçük Mektep Sok.

This church was probably founded towards the end of the 11th century by Anna Dalassene, mother of Alexios I Komnenos who ruled with her son as co-emperor for about 20 years. In 1100 she retired to the convent of the church *St. Saviour* and died there. She was buried in the church in 1105. After *Pantepoptes*

1 Tr. "Yeniçeri, new troops. An organized, paid Turkish military force founded in the 14th century and disbanded in the 19th century.

the capture of Constantinople by the Crusaders in 1204 it remained as a Latin church for 57 years. Alexios had his headquarters near the church and in his hurried flight from the Crusaders he was unable to take his royal pavilion which was immediately occupied by Baudoin of Flanders.[1]

The church is said to have enshrined one of the nails of Christ's cross and several thorns from his crown. These and most of the church relics were sent to Europe, Venice in particular. After the Ottoman conquest it was used as a refectory for a "medrese", a school of Islamic theology, having a soup-kitchen for the poor and students. Later it was turned into a mosque and renamed the Eski İmaret Camii, the Old Soup-Kitchen Mosque.

St. Saviour Pontakrator, The All Powerful
Molla Zeyrek Camii

Location: Fatih, off Atatürk Blvd. at the "Zeyrek" bus stop

This was the largest and the most important Middle Byzantine structure in Constantinople. The church consisted of three separate buildings. The south church was founded by the Empress Irene in the 12th century. The older north church and the funerary chapel between these two churches probably dates from the 10th century. The funerary became the tomb of Manuel I Komnenos and his first wife, Bertha who was the sister-in-law of Conrad, Emperor of Germany. Other members of the Komnenos family and later the Paleologi were buried here also.

During the Latin occupation, the church was robbed of its relics and most of the treasures found their way to St. Mark's Cathedral in Venice. The monastery was taken over by a certain order of monks of St. Anthony. After the fall of the city it was converted to a mosque by Molla[2] Zeyrek

---

1 Count Baldwin of Flanders, the leader of a Crusade that pillaged Constantinople. He was elected the first Latin emperor, a title that remained in his family during the years of the Latin Conquest.
2 A Muslim learned in theology and sacred law of the Koran.

Mehmet Efendi and has ever since been known as "Molla Zeyrek Camii".

Little is left of the church's original decorations. There are floor mosaics in the mosque but they are covered by rugs. The exonarthex at the front of the north church has disappeared but part of it remains before the funerary chapel. The red marble framework of a door of the south church can be seen. The cupolas were rebuilt after the conquest. Until about 1960 the sarcophagus of Irene stood under a wooden covering in the square of the mosque, later to be moved to the Archeological Museum. She was the first to be buried in the church.

In the 12th century it was part of a monastery which had a hospital, a hostelry and a home for the aged. In his book, "Byzantine Churches in Constantinople", Van Milligen gives an interesting description of the monastery. The hospital had 50 beds - ten formed a ward for surgical cases, eight for acute diseases, ten for ordinary maladies and twel-

ve for women. The fifth ward had ten beds and here the patients upon admittance had to wait until the physicians decided on the gravity of the case. Each ward had 2 doctors, 3 medical assistants and 4 aides. In the women's ward there was a female doctor, 6 female surgeonsand 2 female nurses.

All patients were treated gratuitously upon arrival at the hospital. They were given clean clothes, a stipend of food and some money. Doctors made daily rounds of the patients quarters. In addition to the hospital the monastery kept on the same liberal scale a home for old men. Even Gennadius was here before becoming the patriarch. All these have long since disappeared. Ruins remain that may be part of the substructure of these buildings. Parts of the walls of the hospital can be seen from the main road below. They are the remains of the legacy of the hospital's past.

St. Theodore, The Church Mosque
Kilise Camii
Location: Beyazıt, Tirendaz Sok. near Ist. University

The church is believed to have been built in the 11-12 centuries. The existence of a monastery dating from the middle of the 5th century was brought to light during the 1937-38 excavations when the foundations of many walls were found.

It is worth visiting to see the architecture of the narthex that has some interesting capitals, columns and door frames.

After the city's conquest Şeyhulislam Molla Gürani converted it to a mosque. Molla Gürani was a foremost theologian and teacher of Sultan Fatih Mehmet.

St. Mary of Constantinople
Odalar Camii
Location: Draman, Draman Cad., near Kefeli Camii, within walking distance from the Fethiye Camii

This Byzantine church was given to the Dominicans when the church of St. Nicholas was converted to Kefeli

St. Saviour
Pontakrator

Mescidi in 1627. The church possessed a wooden painting of the Virgin of Hodighiterea of St. Luke, which the Dominicans had brought from Kaffa to Constantinople. When it was converted to a mosque in 1636 in the reign of Murat IV, the relic was taken to the Church of SS. Peter and Paul in Galata where it can still be seen.

Because of its numerous chambers (odalar) that made up the substructure of the church and were used by the married Janissaries, it was renamed the "Odalar Camii" during the conversion. A fire destroyed the mosque in 1919 and it was not rebuilt. A playground covers the ruins of this former church and mosque.

Monastery of Gastria
Sancaktar Mescidi

Location: Koca Mustafa Paşa, Sancaktar Tekke Sok., near the Istanbul Hospital

According to legend this monastery was founded by St. Helen in the 4th century. On her return from Jerusalem she brought some flowers from Calvary and planted them in vases (gastria) from which the church derived its name.

On the death of Michael III in 867, his mother the Empress Theodora retired to the monastery with her daughters. Various dates are given for its founding.

The Eastern Catholics a.k.a and the non-Latin Catholics and Their Churches in Istanbul[1]

Father Janin states in his book, "This rapid historical survey shows how complicated is the study of the separated Eastern churches. At first glance it seems difficult to find one's way through this maze of rites, nationalities, beliefs, and hierarchies." These statements could not be truer. So we hope that you will be indulgent with us if you find the information insufficient.

There are a number of ethnological subdivisions of the Eastern Catholics.

The ones that are found in Istanbul are of:

1) The Antiochene[2] rite - The Syrians (Süryani)

2) The Armenian rite - The Armenians

3) The Chaldean rite - The Chaldeans (Kaldi) including a few Melchites[3]

4) The Byzantine rite - The Greek Catholic

---

1 Refers to those Catholics and churches that developed in the eastern half of the Roman Empire plus those groups that were founded and dependent on them, even though they were founded outside the boundaries of the Roman Empire. These churches evolved from the Patriarchates of Constantinople, Alexandria, Antioch, Persia, and Armenia.

2 The original religious rite of the Church of Antioch when Christianity was first established.

3 Oriental Christians whose liturgy is in Arabic. They were also called the "King's Men" because of their loyalty to Constantinople.

The Eastern Catholics are fully in union with the Holy See of Rome belonging to the Uniate[4] rites. In the East whether before or after the schism, clerical celibacy was never a rule for the lower clergy. In these rites, the general law is that a married man may be ordained to the diaconate and priesthood and retain his wife. He may not marry after receiving the diaconate or remarry if his wife dies. Bishops must be single or widowers. For that reason they were formerly chosen from among the monks.

The ancient Christian liturgies are works of art, manifestations of the religious, social and cultural life of the Christian communities over long centuries before Latinization came into effect. Their services have more of a "mysterious" atmosphere and a ritual purely for the sake of its symbolism. The Latin services are conducted with more simplicity. The Eastern Catholic churches do not customarily have organs in their churches. The vestments worn by the clergy deacons etc. are symbolic and of medieval origin. Their original places of worship had no religious statues. These were introduced from the West. Only pictures, wall-paintings and mosaics were permitted.

"The Orientals" as sometimes the Eastern Catholics are referred to, have been accustomed in a large measure to leave the obligations of religion to the individual conscience rather than to make them subjects of positive law. The Eastern Catholics, though small in number, are a very important factor in the union of the Catholic faith.

The Armenian Catholics

This congregation of Christians belongs to the Armenian Rite of the Holy See of Rome. Their liturgy is held in Old Armenian. It is said that their connection dates from 1198. A strong movement which slowly led to the separation

---

4   The churches of the Eastern Christendom in communion with Rome which yet retain their respective languages, rites and canon law

Surp Hovannes,
Armenian
Catholic Church

of the two Armenian churches began with the Dominican missionaries in the 14th century. In 1439 a union with Rome was accepted by the scattered members, who were mostly nobles, of the Armenian church outside of Armenia.

There are the archbishoprics of Mardin, Sivas, Tokat "Constantinople", (all of which are in Turkey), Aleppo (in Syria) and Lvov (the USRR). There are also the Mechitarists of Venice.

This is a congregation of monks whose founder, Mechitar, was born in Sebaste, Armenia in 1676. He formally joined the Latin church in 1701 with 16 companions, forming a religious institute and became its superior. Their united propaganda was opposed by many Armenians so they were compelled to move to Morea, the island of Pelops in Greece, when it was Venetian territory and they built a monastery there in 1706. When hostilities broke out between the Ottomans and the Venetians, they migrated to Venice where they were given the island of St. Lazzaro in 1749. It is still their headquarters where there is a very rich library of various Armenian theological and literary works. Mechitar died at St. Lazzaro in 1749.

The congregation has about 5000 members. The Archbishop of the Armenian Catholics resides in Istanbul with the Archdiocese being at the Church of the Blessed Virgin Mary in Taksim.

Surp Azdvadzadzin (Church of the Blessed Virgin Mary Conception)

Location: Sakızağaç Sok. 31 Taksim, Beyoğlu F[1] 1865 R[2] 1889

The Archdiocese is located in this church.

1 F: Founding date
2 R: Restoration date

Surp Hisus Pirgiç (Church of Christ the Saviour)

Location: Necati Bey Cad. Kuyu Sok. 3-5 Karaköy

As one walks up on the left hand side of the street towards St. Benoit, there is a short set of stairs ending in a courtyard where the church is located. F 1832

This church used to be the bishop's seat before it was transferred to Taksim. Mass is held every Thursday at 10:30 a.m. and on special Holy Days.

Surp Azdvadzadzin Anarad Hiğutyun Church

Location: Samatya Cad. Samatya, F 1839 R 1856

This church is not easily seen from the street because it is behind large iron doors. One enters a small garden. There is another building near the church which is the administrative center of the Foundation of the Armenian Catholics. There are two paintings of interest in the church. One is of St. Gregory the Illuminator with one of the Popes and the other is of the Blessed Gomilas, a martyr.

Surp Hagop Chapel

Location: Cumhuriyet Cad. at the Hospital of St. Jacob, across the street from the Divan Hotel

Surp Hovhannes Vosgeperan (Church of St. John Chrysostom)

Location: Zambak Sok. Taksim, Beyoğlu, F 1837 R 1863

Surp Yerortutuin (Church of the Holy Trinity)

Location: İstiklal Cad. Galatasaray near Odakule, Perükar Çıkmazı No.14 F 1699 R 1770

This church used to be the cathedral of the Catholic community. The cathedral was transferred in later years to the Church of St. Espirit in Elmadağ. At present the interior is in a state of ruin and is being repaired.

Surp Azdvadzadzin Anarad Hiğutyun

Location: Pangaltı, Zafer Sok F 1866 R 1973

Surp Krikor Lusavoriç (Church of St. Gregory the Illuminator)

Location: Dereboyu Cad. 132/2 Ortaköy, F 1839 R 1857

Surp Hovhannes Miğirdiç (Church of St. John the Baptist)

Location: Köybaşı Arka Sok. Yeniköy

Surp Boğos (Church of St. Paul)

Location: Piyasa Cad. Büyükdere, F 1838 R 1885

Surp Boğos, Church of St. Paul

Surp Andon (Church of St. Anthony)
Location: Haziran Sok. Tarabya, F 1871

Surp Levon (Church of St. Leon)
Location: Ali Suavi Sok. 1/3 Kadiköy, F 1911

Surp Azdvadzadzin (Church of the Blessed Virgin Mary)
Location: Büyükada, Mehmetçik Sok., opposite Kanarya Sok, F1858

The Chaldean Catholic Church

There is quite a complicated history of this ancient church which has a glorious past and years of religious conflict. It seems that no history, be it social or religious, is simple, involving as it does continuous power struggles and bitter rivalry which last for centuries. In spite of all this, the Chaldean Catholics have survived and are recognized as one of the canonical rites of the Holy See of Rome. Its members are subject to the Chaldean Patriarch of Babylon, wrongly named so because of an erroneous identification of modern Baghdad with ancient Babylon. The Archdiocese of the Chaldeans is administered by the Archbishop of Diyarbakır (Amida)[1] and the Turkish Chaldeans. His residence is in Istanbul.

Edessa (Urfa) in Southeastern Turkey was the intellectual center of the Christian Orient and the earliest seat of Syriac[2] -speaking Christians. It was here that Addai, a missionary of St. Thomas, converted King Abgar[3] to Christianity in 114 A.D.. Because of theological differences the Syriac-speaking Christians split into two groups; one was the Nestorians[4] or East-Syrians. They were excluded from Edessa

---

1   Diyarbakır, a city in southeastern Turkey
2   A Semitic language of ancient Syria, a branch of Aramaic. It was the language of Edessa that was the centre of Christianity at the end of the 2nd century.
3   One of the kings of Mesopotamia whose capital was Edessa, during the time of Christ. Legend is that he had leprosy and sent a letter to Christ acknowledging his divinity and asking for help, the answer of which Christ sent through one of his disciples.
4   Many controversies arose in the early period of Christianity and this one is worth a few words because of the disputes which resulted from its convictions.

and settled in Nisibis, Persia. The other group was the Jacobites[5] (Monophysites) or West Syrians who remained under the Byzantine influence.

Ethnically the roots of the Chaldeans go back to the Assyrians of Mesopotamia. In the Bible the term Chaldean is synonymous with the Babylonians. The Catholic Chaldeans are the descendants of the East Syrians and Persian Christians who once accepted the heresy of Nestorianism but returned to definite union with Rome in the 16th century when the Chaldean Catholic Church was established. The name "Chaldean" was given by Pope Eugenius IV (1447).

In the rite, Syriac is used in the liturgy although the faithful pray in Arabic or Turkish depending on the area of the country that they come from. The rite has remained basically unchanged for centuries. In the period of union with the Catholic church, few changes were made but no obvious Latinization took place. However, a few changes were found to be necessary in the 16th and 18th centuries. An imitation of the Latin's genuflection was adopted. They have preserved their traditions up to the present day.

The monk, Nestorius, who was the Patriarch of Constantinople in 428 and Cyril, the Patriarch of Alexandria had a serious dispute about the two natures (human and divine) in Christ. The humanity of Christ was over-emphasized by Nestorius and he did not agree with the traditional description of Mary as Theotokos, the Mother of God but called her the Mother of Christ since she was the mother of the human form alone. So an argument resulted between the two patriarchs with Rome siding against what were considered the pretentious claims of upstarts in Constantinople. Here is seen the entry of politics into religious affairs. The two emperors, Theodosios II of the East an Valentinian III of the West called the third general council of the Church of Ephesus in 431 which condemned Nestorianism and exiled Nestorius to the Egyptian desert in 435.

However the Christian School of Edessa was transferred to Nisibis in 489. Nestorius continued his teachings there and was supported by the Persian King. Missionaries went as far as China and for centuries they were a recognized institution in Islamic lands.

During the 16th century various attempts were made to promote union with Rome but they were largely fruitless. By the 18th century a large section of this group joined Rome as the Chaldean Catholic Church. After W.W.I. many Nestorians moved to San Francisco.

5   A sect of Monophysites deriving their name from James Baradeus (d. 578) a bishop of Edessa who organized their church.

The Turks of the congregation have settled in isolated villages in the Southeastern part of Turkey such as Maraş, Urfa and Mardin. Over the years due to social changes and for economic reasons, many have moved to Istanbul. Due to the West's increasing interest in Eastern Christianity many have gone abroad.

A few Melchite families belong to this congregation. Services are held every Sunday morning at 10:30 in the crypt of St. Anthony's Church in Galatasaray. Monsignor Paul Karataş who served as a consultant in deciphering the Hammurabi Code[1] that is to be found in the British Museum, is the Archbishop of the Turkish Chaldeans.

Church of Saint Panteleemon (Pantaleon)

Location: Sakızağacı Sok. 55/1, Beyoğlu

We found this church accidentaly when wandering in the back streets of Beyoğlu and Tarlabaşı. We noticed a building that had a cross on its door and were tempted to open it. We did so and entered a small hall where, hanging on the wall, was a picture of a saint and Greek letters on the picture. There was a box of candles beneath the painting. There was another door to be opened and on going through we found ourselves in a church. It looked like a Catholic church with its altar, pews, a Madonna and other religious paintings.

Then a young girl appeared from a gallery upstairs. She was dressed typically as the women of Southeastern Turkey do. She was wearing a colourful blouse, a long skirt and a white-beaded scarf which was wrapped in a different style around her head. She said that the priest was upstairs and went to call him. A man in his thirties came down and unlike the rest of the family who came down to look at us and were speaking an Arabic dialect among themselves, spoke to

---

1 One of the first set of condified laws from the 19th century B.C. that came from Mesopotamia. It was engraved in cuneiform characters on an eight foot column of hard stone. It is in the British Museum.

us in Turkish. He said that he also spoke French. From his willing answers to our questions we learned that most of the Chaldeans had come about 60 years ago from Southeastern Turkey. He showed us an old handwritten Aramaic bible using Arabic script and read to us from it. There was a congregation that met everyday at 17:00 for Mass which is celebrated in Aramaic. This church was given to the Chaldeans by the Greeks and that is why there is Greek script writing on the painting of St. Panteleemon.

The Greek Catholic of the Byzantine Rites

This congregation of Catholics who are under the Holy See of Rome came from Anatolia in 1861. The majority of them moved to Greece just before World War II. Today there are a very few families left. There is only one priest in Istanbul who is an Archimandrite or Father Superior.

The Hagia Triada (The Church of the Holy Trinity)

Location: Galatasaray, Hamalbaşı Cad. 44, in the neighbourhood of the British Consulate

It is located in a large building which used to be a Greek primary school. As you walk down towards Tepebaşı you will see a green door with a cross on it. On entering one finds a small church similar to a Greek Orthodox church. Services are held in Greek every morning including Sundays.

The Syrian Catholics

There were many struggles among the ancient Christian groups as they started to develop in the Near East. One such internal dispute existed within the Christian Syrians. One group was the Jacobites or the Syrian Monophysite Church who wanted to be named the Syrian Orthodox Church. The other group, the Syrian Catholics were those Jacobites who returned to union with the Holy See of Rome.

The Patriarchal throne of Antioch often changed hands between the two groups. Emperor Justinian I finally imprisoned all the Monophysite bishops. But his wife, the Empress Theodora, favoured the latter and in about 543 A.D. sent a priest Jacob Baradeus to secretly reorganize them.

Then for centuries the shuffling goes on. Before his death in 1783, the ancient Syrian Patriarch of Antioch appointed as his succesor Michael Jarweh, the Archbishop of Aleppo, who had just become a Catholic.

His patriarchal residence was in Mardin. While Michael was on a visit to the Pope in Rome, an anti-Catholic group elected another patriarch who was recognized by the Ottoman government.

Upon returning to Mardin Michael was imprisoned by the newly elected patriarch. Michael escaped, first to Baghdad and then to a monastery in Lebanon from where he governed his followers until his death in 1801. Michael Jarweh is recognized as the first patriarch of Antioch of the Syrian Catholics. In 1830 the patriarchate moved to Aleppo and was recognized by the Ottoman government. After a brief period it moved to Mardin and finally was established in Beirut.

The liturgy of this rite is in "Edessene" a dialect of Syriac or Aramaic, the language of Christ. This ancient liturgical language is only used by the priest when he says mass. Since the language is no longer understood by many, the introductional part of the Bible, the sermons and other prayers recited by the congregation were in Arabic in the past.

Church of the Sacred Heart

Location: Saray Arkası Sok. Ayazpaşa, Taksim (at the back of the German Consulate)

This church and its monastery were built in 1922 and used to belong to the Jesuits. It was given to the Syrian Catholic community in 1983. Up to that date the community used a church in Gedikpaşa, Beyazıt which had belonged to

Church of the Sacred Heart

the Assumptionists. At present this church belongs to the "Süryani Kadim" community.

The Church of the Sacred Heart is under the administration of Monsignor Yusuf Sağ. There are two lovely chapels, meeting rooms and administrative offices in the building. Pope John XXIII stayed here at the time when he was the Apostolic Vicar and Delegate in Turkey. Now the prayers have been transcribed to Turkish because most of the church members are unfamiliar with the ancient language that had been used in the services.

Services are held at 11:00 on Sundays in the winter and at 10:00 in the summer.

The Latin Catholics and
Their Curches in Istanbul

The first Latins were the Venetians settling in Galata during Justinian's reign in the 7th century. They were given commercial rights in the capital in 991 A.D. The Pisans were given the same privleges in 1112 which were also granted to the Genoeses in 1152.

Internal struggles soon resulted among them and these were encouraged by the Byzantines who massacred some of the Latins. Trade negotiations were entered into by Alexios V Doukas with the 4th Crusaders but all in vain. This Crusade was a Venetian enterprise for they wanted control of the trade that passed through the city. They succeeded in capturing Constantinople in 1204. After 3 days of massacre and pillage a Latin Kingdom was established by Baldwin of Flanders (Baldwin I of the Latin Empire) who was crowned emperor by the papal delegate in Hagia Sophia on May 16, 1204. The Latin Church rite was officially introduced in all the Byzantine churches although the Orthodox creed was practised secretly. A papal legate officiated at Hagia Sophia. The existing convents were filled with Latin religious orders and the Church of the Pontakrator became an imperial residence.

After the Greek restoration of 1261 the Latins were forced to return to their pre-conquest churches, most of which do not exist today. Due to the bitter feelings resulting with the Venetian Crusaders, only some Latins were privileged to remain in Galata. With the Ottoman Conquest of 1453 they again lost their privileges with only some Maltese and Franks (a name given to all foreigners) who chose to remain.

For many years the Catholics were unable to build any new churches but in the last few years many churches are being restored and decorated. The Catholics here belonging to the Holy See of Rome are known as the "Latin Catholics". Many of the churches have a booklet that lists the times of their services.

The Dominicans

They are a religious order founded in 1215 in Toulouse, France. They are also called the Friar Preachers and in England, the Black Friars because of the black mantle that they wear over a white habit. Their founder, St. Dominic, was a Castillian by birth. The order was established to serve as preachers and work among the heretics of that time. They are a body of highly trained priests, devoted to preaching and teaching.

The Dominicans are among the earliest religious order to be established in Constantinople. They used to have the churches of St. Nicholas (Kefeli Camii) St. Theodosia (Gül Camii), St. Paul and St. Dominic (Arap Camii) and the Convent of Manuel. They now have the following three churches:

Church of SS. Peter and Paul

Location: Kuledibi Sok. 44, Galata - a short distance from the Galata Tower

This is one of the surviving medieval Latin churches to be found in Istanbul. When the Dominican fathers were turned out of St. Paul's (Arap Camii) by the Grenadines in 1535, the order was taken under the protection of a Venetian noble, Signor Angelo Zaccaria who owned property around this church. This nobleman was a patron of the neighbouring chapel of SS. Peter and Paul which was the house of worship of an order of nuns from the convent of St. Catherine. On April 20, 1535 he conceded the chapel with all the property dependent on it, to the Dominicans on the condition that they lit a candle for him on the Feast of the Purification of the Blessed Virgin (Feb.2, Candlemas) and celebrated a mass for him and his relatives every week.

The Church was rebuilt in 1603-04 and by a royal decree of Sultan Ahmet I in 1608 it was placed under the protection of France. In 1660 a fire destroyed both the church and the convent. According to the law at the time, neither could be rebuilt and the site reverted to the government. However, later due to the good will of the government the church was finally rebuilt.

Between 1702 and 1706 it became exclusively the French parochial church of Galata. Up to that date the church also had an annual subsidy from Venice which was later withdrawn because the Dominicans opposed the removal to Venice of a relic of the sacred image of the Hodighitria. This is a painting of the Virgin, the appointed protectress of Byzantium. In 1536 it was in the Dominican Church of the Virgin Rosary, later to be brought to SS. Peter and Paul.

In 1731 the great fire of Galata destroyed the church which was immediately rebuilt on the same site. This church was built entirely of wood and lasted until 1841 when it was rebuilt in its present form by the Swiss architect, Fossati.

There is a variety of relics in the church, such as a portion of the bones of St. Rene said to have been brought from the catacombs, relics of St. Thomas, St. Dominic, St. Catherine of Sienna and of St. Hyacinth[1] . Over the small altar to the left of the main one is the famous painting. It was resto-

1 A Polish Dominican friar whose missionary work extended as far as Constantinople. He died in Krakow in 1257 and his feast day is Aug. 17.

red in about 17th century since all that remained of the original were the head and chest. The remainder of the picture is enclosed in a decorative metallic covering.

On entering the small courtyard, one can see some armorial bearings from France, tombstones of some Maltese families and burial crypts. At the rear one can still see part of an old Genoese wall.

Week-day masses are at 08:00, Sundays and holy days at 11:00 . The feast day of SS. Peter and Paul is June 29.

Church of Notre Dame de Rosarie

Location: Kapamacı Ekrem Sok. 24, Bakırköy

This is quite a large church for the small community that attends services here. Belonging to the Dominican order, it was built over a century ago by a generous donation from an Italian family that lived in Istanbul. The church has been repainted recently. The Syrian "Kadim" (ancient Syrian) also use the church.

Services are held in Turkish. Daily masses are at 18:30 and Sundays at 11:00.

Church of the Blessed Virgin Mary

Location: Samatya, not far from Imrahor Camii

This church is being used by the Syrian Orthodox community.

The Assumptionists

This Roman Catholic religious congregation of men also known as the Augustinians of the Assumption, was founded by by Rev. Edmond d'Alzon in 1843 in Nimesin, France. Its members are engaged in teaching, parochial, ministrial and missionary work, the social apostolate and dissemination of literature especially in the interest of Christian unity. In the field of scholarship they specialize in Byzantine theology. The headquarters is in Rome.

Church of Notre Dame de L'Assumption

Location: Cem Sok.5, Moda-Kadıköy

This is one of the most beautiful churches of Istanbul. It was built in 1859 under an imperial decree and took the name of "St. Euphemia of Chalcedonia".

When the Assumptionists were established here the church was renamed. According to the R.C. Church it is an article of faith that although she died naturally, the Blessed Virgin Mary, at the end of her life was taken to heaven body and soul. The feast day of her Assumption is Aug. 15.

Summer weekly services are at 19:00, winter until the end of May at 18:30, on Sundays at 8:00 on Saturdays at 11:00, the services are in Turkish.

Church of St. Augustine

Location: Atlı Han Sok.1, Fenerbahçe-Kadıköy

Every first Sunday of the month the services are at 10:00 in Turkish.

The Franciscan Orders

St. Francis of Assisi (1182-1226), the son of a rich merchant, having renounced all his riches, founded a religious order which he wanted solidly established on poverty and humility, calling it the Order of the Friars Minor or Little Brothers. Down through the centuries different reforms took shape and came into being as a result of the urge for a return to the primitive observance of poverty.

There were some reforms in the original order and at present the Franciscan Order is divided into three fully autonomous families. They are commonly known as the Friars Minor (O.F.M.), Friars Minor Conventual (O.F.M. Conv.) and Friars Minor Capuchin (O.F.M. Cap.) These orders are closely united in spirit and collaborate in the fields of pastoral, cultural, social, and other activities.

The Franciscans were among the first religious Order to come to Constantinople in the first decades of the 13th century during the Latin occupation.

Some Friars were certainly in the city in 1219, but the first Franciscan residence was established in 1221, when they were assigned the Byzantine church of the Theotokos (Mother of God) Kyriotissa, later converted into a mosque under the name of Kalenderhane Camii.

Church of St. Anthony of Padua

Location: İstiklal Cad., No.325, Galatasaray, Beyoğlu. It is just a few minutes walk from Galatasaray Lycee, towards Tünel.

The Franciscans first came to Constantinople in 1221. Their first residence was at the church of Theotokos Kyriotissa. During a period of restoration they built a friary adjacent to a church in Galata that was dedicated to St. Francis. This church was referred to in literature as the St. Sophia of the Latins. Fatih never wanted it to be converted to a mosque. Unfortunately it fell prey to arson three times in 1639, 1660 and 1696 never to be rebuilt again.

Deprived of their century old residence, the Franciscans conventuals moved to Pera where they owned a small vineyard and a country-house attached to a small wooden chapel dedicated to St. Anthony. On these grounds they built a more spacious wooden church, which took the place of the original chapel, consecrated and officially opened in 1724. Destroyed by fire in 1762, it was rebuilt again in 1763 to be burnt down once more in 1831. Reconstruction work was immediately taken up and a slightly bigger church came into being. And this time it was to stay until the beginning of the century, when it was demolished to make possible the widening of the Rue de Pera, the present Istiklal Caddesi. So, in 1905, the Friars bought the site of the old Teatro della Concordia, burnt down some years before, and started preparing the plans for the new church. The first stone was blessed and laid on August 23, 1906.

The construction was completed in 1913 and the church was officially opened on November 16 of the same year. St.

Church of St. Anthony of Padua

Anthony's Basilica, the last Catholic church to be built in Turkey and the largest existing Christian church in Istanbul, in neo-gothic style, is the work of Giulio Mongeri and Edoardo De Nari, two very reknown architects at the turn of the century. The church, which has the biggest pipe organ in Turkey is the venue for organ recitals by world famous organists and in particular the ones organised by the Istanbul Arts and Music Festival. It is also the church where the first Pope ever to visit Turkey, Paul VI, in 1967, celebrated his first Mass on Turkish soil. A plaque commemorating the event can be seen in the chapel on the righthand side of the main altar. Here also, Mgr. A.G. Roncalli, Papal Delegate to Turkey and Greece, later Pope John XXIII, on June 13, 1940, the feastday of St. Anthony invoked the intercession of the Saint for the safety of Istanbul and Turkey from the horrors of war. In October 1987 the closing ceremony of the Ecumenical Congress commemorating the 12th centenary of the II Council of Nicea was held here. It is the most popular church in Istanbul with people of all faiths visiting it. Masses are said in English at 10, in Italian at 11, in Polish at 12 and at 19:00 (summer) and 18:00 (winter) in Italian on Sundays and feastdays. On weekdays mass is said in the evening as above according to the season. Besides on Tuesdays, at 11:30 Mass and special devotions to St. Anthony are held in Turkish. The feast of the Saint is celebrated on June 13. Confessions can be heard in English, Italian, French and Polish.

Church of the Nativity of the Blessed Virgin Mary

Location: Azaplı Sokak, Büyükdere, Sarıyer

In 1807 the Franciscan Conventuals had a small wooden church on the Bosphorus in Büyükdere. As there was a flourishing Italian community in that area, the Friars thought of building a bigger church of stone dedicated to the Nativity of the Blessed Virgin Mary, and it was ready for worship in 1866. Most of the Italians living in the surrounding area were mason and marble workers engaged in various work on the imperial buildings and very willingly not only contributed but also worked themselves to make the dream come true. It has some very nice paintings by a Sicilian artist, Giuseppe Carta. The ceiling depicting the Immaculate Conception of the Blessed Virgin is a real masterpiece by the same painter. It has a large pleasant garden. The Friary was partly restored in 1984/5 and is now the residence of a Secular Institute known as Focolare whose specific mission is to promote Christian Unity. Mass is said in Italian every Sunday and on feastdays at 10:30 .

Church of the Nativity of the Blessed Virgin Mary

Church of St. Louis des Francais

Location: Postacılar Sok.11 Beyoğlu, on the grounds of the French Consulate

The present chapel is the oldest Latin church in Pera[1]. France was the first European nation to establish formal diplomatic relations with the Ottoman Empire beginning with envoys sent by Francois I to the court of Süleyman the Magnificent in 1525. In 1581 the French ambassador, Chevalier of Greminy, found Galata too crowded and built a palace among the "Vines of Pera". In 1628, the ambassador installed some Capuchins in the chapel next to the embassy.

A school for French children was opened on the grounds, and in 1660 a church was added. A "Language School for the Young", was founded in 1665 and directed by the Capuchins. The intention was to teach oriental languages to young men, at first the French and later the Levantines[2], with a view of placing the students as dragomen in the French missions of the Levant.

The church was built of stone in 1788, but it burned down in 1831. For a short time in 1917 it was used as a mosque for the children of the Home for Turkish Orphans which had been established in the school. In 1918 it resumed its former function as a Roman Catholic church. Many French ambassadors are interred here.

It is said that a famous Turkish astronomer and mathematician established an observatory on these grounds but it was destroyed in 1579.

Church of St. Etienne

Location: Cümbüş Sok. No.12, Yeşilköy

Until 1924 this district of Istanbul was known as Ayastafanos (St. Stephen-St. Etienne)

*Church of the
Nativity of the
Blessed Virgin Mary*

1 The European quarter of Constantinople, now known as Beyoğlu, and was so called during the pre-republic period of Istanbul.
2 Used to describe the people of the Mediterranean coastline. In Turkey it is used to describe families whose origin is Italian, French and Spanish.

Masses are held every weekday at 08:00 - 19:00 on Holy days and on Sundays at 08:00 and 10:30

Church of St. Mary Draperis

Location: İstiklal Cad. 429, Beyoğlu near Tünel. It can easily be found because there is a set of stairs that goes down from the street level.

At the beginning of 1453 the Franciscans of the Observance had completed their church of St. Anthony of the Cypresses which was near Sirkeci, but with the Turkish conquest they were forced to abandon that district. They wandered about the city for some time till they finally settled in the Mumhane quarter of Galata where a certain Clara Bertola Draperis gave them a house where a small chapel was built to shelter a precious painting on wood of the Virgin. The chapel burnt down in 1660 but the painting was saved by the Draperis family. In 1678 the Franciscans established themselves in Pera. The new church burnt down in 1700, was rebuilt, only to be destroyed by an earthquake. Again it was rebuilt, to be burnt down once more.

The present church dates from 1789. The painting of the Virgin that was miraculously saved from all these catastrophes may be seen above the main altar.

Masses are held every morning at 08:00, on Thursdays at 08:00 and 09:00 and on Sundays at 09:00 and 11:30.

Church of St. Pacifique

Location: Yeni Sok., Büyükada

Masses are held on weekdays at 20:30, on Holy days at 18:00, on Sundays at 11:00 but in the summer at 10:30

Chapel of the Terre Sainte (Holy Land, Our Lady of Seven Sorrows)

Location: Postacılar Sok. Beyoğlu. As you walk down from Galatasaray towards Tünel, take the sixth street on the left, walk to the end of the street, take a right turn and it will be directly in front of you.

The Terre Sainte belonged to the former Spanish Em-

Church of St. Mary Draperis

bassy in Istanbul. The Spanish Franciscans of the Observance who founded a convent near St. Marie Draperis in 1670 had services there. The present chapel dates from 1871. It is no longer active but services are held there on special occasions.

The Lazarists

This is a Catholic society of priests founded by St. Vincent de Paul in 1625. Their official title is the "Congregation of the Mission". In 1632 they were given the priory of St. Lazarus in Paris and so were known as the Lazarists. They are also referred to as the Vincentians. They are engaged in secondary and university education as well as pastoral and charitable works. The following groups are found in Istanbul.

The Austrian Lazarists at:

The Church of St. George

Location: Kartçınar Sok. 6 of Bankalar Cad., Galata

Services are held every Sunday at 09:30 and on Wednesdays at 18:30

This church appears to be the most ancient church in Galata because it existed in the first centuries of Christianity in Byzantium. Its origin must belong to the same period as the Ayazma of St. Irene that is to be found in the church. It is said that St. Irene consecrated the church herself.

During the reorganization of the suburb of Galata in 1303, a church of St. George is referred to as being in the neighbourhood but no mention is made of the creed practiced there. The probability is that it was originally Greek and given over to the Latins in 1349. In turn it has been served by the Jesuits (1585), the Dominicans (and the French Capuchins 1626). In 1660 it was destroyed by a fire and not rebuilt till 1667. Then in 1696 the church and in 1731 the convent were destroyed by fire. The church was rebuilt in 1731 with donations from Louis XV of France and this is the present-day building.

The Capuchins sold the church to the Apostolic Vicarate which resold it to the Bosnian Franciscan Observants in 1853. The convent has since become a hospital.

Finally in 1882, the Austrian Lazarists bought St. George's and founded a school for girls and boys next to the church. The school was intended for children of the minority groups living in the city. In 1917 when Turkish became an obligatory language in the schools, Turkish children were also admitted.

The French Lazarists at:

The Chapel of the Sacre Coeur

Location: Yoğurtçu Zülfü Sok.15, Bebek

Masses are held at 10:30 every Sunday

The Sisters of Charity of St. Vincent de Paul or the Sisters of Charity as they are commonly called, are a congregation of nuns founded by Louise de Marillac who, encouraged by St. Vincent de Paul, established an order to undertake charitable works.

The French branch of the Sisters of Charity have the following establishments in Istanbul. The school of St. Benoit (see the Church of St. Benoit), a hospital "La Paix" in Şişli, and a school for girls "St. Pulcherie" on Çukurlu Çeşme Sok. 7, Parmakkapı, Beyoğlu.

The Italian Sisters of Charity of the Immaculate Conception have a school for girls on Turnacıbaşı Sok. 30 in Beyoğlu and the Italian Hospital on Defterdar Yokuşu in Cihangir.

Church of St. Benoit (St. Benedict)

Location: Kemeraltı Cad. 35, Karaköy

The exact date of the foundation of the church is unknown but records show that it dates back to at least Pope Urban V (1362-1379) having been built by the Republic of

Genoa after the destruction of a Genoese church in Constantinople, that was called St. Michael's. For a long time St. Benoit's was known as the "Church of the Genoese". It was built outside the walls of Galata during the 14th century and was midst the Greek and Armenian quarter.

The church was a kind of stronghold with its belfry built in the style of the Crusaders "Keep and Watch" tower and crenalated walls. It was dedicated to the Virgin Mary and St. Benoit.

The Benedictines were in Constantinople before the Latin conquest in which they had also taken part and did not install themselves at St. Benoit's until 1450, three years before the Turkish conquest. Up to the 17th century a convent of St. Mary Misericorde existed in the precints. The church was served successively by the Benedictines, the Franciscan Observants and after 1583 by the Jesuits who built and opened a school in the annexes of the convent. The church was completely restored with numerous mosaics in 1610.

A French historian when visiting this part of the world from 1546-1549 wrote that he had seen the remains of a great cistern supported by 300 columns on the premises. When the Moors[1] of Granada were expelled from Spain, Süleyman the Magnificent wished to convert the church to a mosque, but through the intervention of King Francois I in 1540 the church became the royal chapel of the French ambassador.

In the 1660 Galata fire the church was spared but other fires destroyed it in 1686 and 1696. The Latin inscriptions in the church describe these fires. The columns that embelish the top of the stairway to the church were given by the müftü[2] who granted the right that was reserved only for

1 A Muslim people of mixed Berber and Arab race who inhabited NW. Africa and conquered Spain in the 8th century. In 1569 the Spanish Moors emigrated in part, revolted in part and were driven out of Spain at which time a number of them came to this part of the world.
2 A Muslim official representative who interprets religious law.

mosques to have a lead roof built on the church. This was a period of great importance of the church. Frank, Greek and Armenian rites were observed in rotation and sermons were given in French, Italian, Turkish, Greek and Armenian. With permission from the French ambassador, the German Catholics who did not have their own church at that time held their religious services here, too.

The church was destroyed again with a great part of Galata in 1731 and was rebuilt in the following years. In 1783 ten years after the Brief of Clement XIV had been issued, suppressing the Jesuit order, St. Benoit and all other institutions of the Jesuits were taken over by the Lazarists.

The Lazarists obtained complete ownership of the church in 1802. In 1839 the Sisters of Charity were brought from France and they opened a school for girls. Again in 1865 a fire destroyed part of the church. It was restored and the school was enlarged in 1871.

The church today is a mixture of three construction periods. "The Keep" which shelters bells from the 14th century and the columned portal on Kemeraltı Cad. are of the same period. The nave and the right lateral nave in the church date from 1732. Clumsy restoration in 1871 did away with many of the elegant inscriptions that were found there.

Many French ambassadors, the Princess Tekeli[1], Count Ragotski[2], and other notable personages have memorial stone inscriptions in the church. Many Hungarians stop by to pay homage to Ragotski. Flowers and small flags are always to be found on his memorial.

---

1 Helene Zrinyi and the mother of Count Rakoczy.
2 Count Francis 1676-1735: A Hungarian nobleman who tried to restore independence from the Austrians for the Transylvanians. In 1717 he accepted an offer from Sultan Ahmet III to help organize an army in Turkey against the Austrians. But before reaching Constantinople the Sultan had changed his mind. He was exiled to Tekirdağ in 1719 and remained there until his death on Good Friday in 1735. His remains were solemnly transferred to Hungary in 1906. There is a museum in Tekirdağ dedicated to his memory.

The Salesians

This is a popular name for the Society of St. Francis de Sales, a congregation of Catholic priests and brothers founded by St. John Bosco in Turin, Italy during the 19th century for the care and education of boys and younger men, particularly among the poor. He actively promoted industrial schools and evening schools to develop secular vocations. Pastoral services are carried out by this congregation in the following churches:

Church of Our Lady of Lourdes: Notre Dame de Lourdes, Eglise Georgienne

Location: Kâzım Orbay Cad. 29, Bomonti

A Georgian religious group, the Order of the Immaculate Conception, who came to Istanbul from Russia in the 19th century founded the church in 1861 and restored it in 1901. There are no longer any Georgians connected to the church. The schedule of masses varies as follows:

October-May-mornings at 09:00, Saturdays at 11:30.

June-September, mornings at 08:30, Saturdays at 18:30.

Sundays and Holy days at 08:30 and 11:00.

The Cathedral of St. Esprit

Location: Cumhuriyet Cad. 205/8, Harbiye, near the school of Notre Dame de Sion

When the church was built in 1846, it became the Metropolitan church in Istanbul. Then on Jan. 20, 1876 it was declared a cathedral by a Pontifical Bull. The office of the Papal Representative is attached to the cathedral. There are relics of some early Christian martyrs in the church such as St. Laurence, St. Crispin Pomponius, St. Sebastian and of St. Linus, the first Bishop of Rome after Peter. In the church entrance there are always bulletins of the current church activities in the city. Catholicism lessons are given here for the Catholics.

Weekday and Sunday services are at 09:00 in French and in English at 10:00 on Sundays.

The German Catholic Congregation

The first German priest on record was a Dominican who lived in the Monastery of St. Paul in 1232. Then in 1307 there was a German Franciscan priest in the same monastery. Documents mention that in 1453 a German Franciscan Minor lived and worked at St. Maria Draperis. When St. Anthony's was consecrated in Pera in 1724 German fathers were also there. Most of them came from the south of Germany. Between 1583-1783 there were German speaking fathers at St. Benoit although the administration had been taken over by the French Lazarists in 1733. In 1841 a home for the elderly, "The Antigiana" was founded by Sultan Abdul Mecit (1839-1861) in Harbiye. A chapel was completed on the grounds in 1871. Both the home and the chapel were administered by the Sisters of Charity and Catholics of different heritages were able to live here. Today a committee administers the Antigiana. In 1953 the Papal Secretary gave the German Catholic community permission to use the chapel which was named St. Paul.

Further information can be obtained from The German Catholic Center - Büyük Çiftlik Sok. 14 - Nişantaşı.

Church of St. Paul
Location: Cumhuriyet Cad., Selbaşı Sok., 5 Harbiye
Services are held on Sundays and Holy days at 10:30.

A Latin Church That Became a Mosque

St.Paul and St. Dominic
Arap Camii

Location: Just off Perşembe Pazarı Cad. towards Azapkapı, Karaköy

Muslima, a Muslim general during the Arab seige of Constantinople in 715, is said to have constructed this mosque during the seven year period that he had occupied Galata. Some authors think that it was a church dedicated to a St. Aerobindus, and then renamed the "Arab Mosque" during Muslima's period. It is not exactly known if it remained in the hands of the Muslims after the Arab seige from 739-780. Some Greek writers say that the mosque was taken by the Greeks before the Latin Conquest[1]. But it is certain that during the period of the Latin Empire of the Orient, this edifice was given to St. Hyacinth in 1232. It then either took the place of or included a chapel to St. Pàul as it was popularly known then. The church was completely rebuilt in a Latin architectural style, resembling the Dominican convents in Chiari and Finale, Italy. A belfry was installed at the front of the church on its pointed roof, both of which can be very clearly seen from the main street. After the reoccupation of the city from the Latins in 1261, it still remained in the hands of the Dominicans. According to the custom of that period many personages were buried beneath the flags-

1   By the Crusaders from 1204-1261 A.D.

tone that were garnished with funerary inscriptions and armorial bearings. In 1453 Mehmet the Conqueror allowed
the Dominicans to keep the church and only requisitioned
its bells. The Moors took the church after their exodus from
Spain, reestablishing it again as the "Arab Mosque".

In 1913 when many mosques were being rebuilt, the
wooden flooring was taken up and the Dominican pavings
were discovered. A great number of the flagstones were sent
to the Museum of Archeology and can be seen there in the
Christian room. No traces of the first Arab period can be fo-
und in the present building. Some sculptured moldings and
the general plan of the Latin period can be seen. If one ro-
ams through that neighbourhood, many old buildings dating
back to those periods can still be seen.

*St. Paul and St.
Dominic*

History of The Orthodox and Their Churches

The Armenian Gregorian Church

After Trdat the Great was converted to Christianity in 303 A.D. (some say 280 A.D.) by St. Gregory the Illuminator also called the Apostle of Armenia and the Enlightener, Armenia was the first nation to become Christian. Up to then the Armenians had worshipped the Persian gods. Some historians ascribe the first Christian preaching to SS. Thaddeus and Bartholomew, both who had suffered martyrdom. But the main missionary work was carried out by St. Gregory (240-332).

Some references state that Gregory was an Armenian notable who ran away from Persian oppresion and sought asylum in the Roman town of Caesarea (Kayseri) in Cappadocia. Others say that he was the son of a Parthian[1] who had assasinated King Khosrov I of Armenia and for safety was taken to Caesarea.

There he had a Christian and Greek education, married and had two sons. He was ordained a priest and consecrated as a bishop by Leontios of Caesarea in 302.

---

1 An ancient country southeast of the Caspian Sea. It was inhabited by an Iranian tribe. Much of its history is connected with Persia.

In 313 A.D. the Edict of Milan announced the toleration of Christianity throughout the Roman Empire. So for a time the Armenian church was subservient to Rome. The patriarchate that Gregory had established was hereditary for almost a century and upon his death his son, Aristakes, was appointed Katolikos[2] of the Armenian creed.

St. Gregory preached the new faith in the Armenian language but for nearly a century after their religious conversion, the Armenians had to rely on Greek and Syriac religious texts which were unintelligible to the common man. St. Mesrop, the Teacher, invented the Armenian alphabet at the beginning of the 5th century (404 A.D.) and this helped to strengthen the feeling of national unity. With his principal colleague, St. Isaac (the Great St. Sahak) and encouraged by King Vramshpuh (392-414) a school of translators was formed to translate Syriac and Greek religious works into Armenian.

In the 5th century the verdict of the Fourth Council of Chalcedon in 451, was not accepted by the Armenian church since they had no representatives at the meeting when the theological decisions were being made, but there may have been other reasons involved too. Like the Syrian Orthodox and the Egyptian Copts they believed that the human nature of Christ was absorbed in the divine. This view alienated them from other Christians of that time.

The non-Catholics of this creed are the Gregorians. Their liturgy is in old Armenian. Bishops are chosen from the monks who are the priests that wear black hoods during the services. Their liturgical ceremony developed separately from that of the Greek church and has an individual character strikingly oriental and somewhat quaint according to

2 Universal - this title was held by the primates of the Georgian and Armenian churches and of the Nestorians in Mesopotamia. In the period of the undivided church it was given to the main bishop in a particular region who was directly under the patriarch. With the emergence of the independent churches, Katholikos came to mean the same as Partriarch.

Greek and Western ideas. Be they Uniate (R.C.) or Orthodox the churches of the East glory in having their origins from the apostles themselves. They have maintained a treasury of liturgy, music and spiritual traditions right from the beginning.

The church maintains the 7 Sacraments[1] though extreme unction has fallen out of use. There are no statues in their churches and unleavened bread and wine are not mixed with water for Holy Communion. During Mass an instrument similar to an Egyptian sistrum[2] is jingled.

The altar is not concealed behind a screen but during the more solemn parts of the service, a curtain is drawn.

There are four patriarchates, two of which have the dignity of Katholikos, The Supreme Katolicate who resides in Soviet Armenia has the right to consecrate priests. The Katholikos of Sis (Kozan) resides in Beirut. The other two are the patriarchs of Jerusalem and "Constantinople", the latter keeping the pre-conquest historical name. The church accepts the decisions of the first three ecumenical councils as a definition of its faith. It retains the Julian[3] calendar. The church celebrates Christmas simply as part of the Epiphany[4] on Jan.6. Most of the churches are named after Armenian saints though one will see that there are many who are recognized in common with the other Christian churches.

The church music is quite important in Armenian li-

1 1.Baptism 2.Confirmation 3. Penance 4. The Eucharist 5. Extreme Unction 6. Marriage 7. Ordination
2 A jingling instrument of thin metal, the frame with transverse metal rods and a handle by which it is shaken.
3 Introduced in 46 B.C. by Julius Caesar in which the ordinary year has 365 days and every fourth year, leap year, has 366 days. The order and names of the months and the number of days in each are retained in the modern Gregorian calendar with some modifications introduced to bring it into closer conformity with astronomical data.
4 The commemoration of the Baptism of Christ on Jan. 6. Much can be written on this subject. In Antioch as late as about 386 A.D. Epiphany and Easter were two great feasts and the physical Birth of Christ was not yet celebrated. On the eve of the Epiphany after nightfall the springs and rivers were blessed and water drawn from them was stored for the whole year to be used in lustrations (purification ceremonies) and baptism.

Armenian
Gregorian Chapel

turgy. The choirs of most of the Armenian churches are quite impressive and well worth listening to. Services are held in the churches on Sundays and holy days.

Surp Kevork (St.George)

Formerly called Church of St. Mary Perivlepte - The All - Seeing. Also known as: Sulu Manastır, The Water Monastery F 1031 R 1804

On the same grounds there is also Surp Hovhannes Migirdiç Ayazma Şapeli - The Chapel of the Holy Spring of St. John.

Location: Marmara Cad., Kocamustafapaşa

A church had been constructed here in 1031 by Romanos III Argyros and the repaired by Nikephoros III Botaneites (1078-1081). Both these emperors are said to be buried here. Michael Palaiologos had it carefully restored and at Candlemas all the court went to church with great pomp.

Before the 1782 fire a painting of Michael, his wife Theodora with their son Constantine between them, could be seen in the church. It continued to be a Christian sanctuary even after the Turkish conquest of 1453.

Sultan İbrahim gave the church to the Armenians in 1643. Tales relate that as a result of an intrigue in the harem, one of the sultan's favourites, an Armenian called "A Piece of Sugar" - Şeker Parça, used her influence to make the sultan give the church to the Armenians. According to the published works of the traveler, Simeon of Zamosc, Poland, the church was already in the hands of the Armenians in 1608 and had served as the cathedral of the Armenian patriarchate.

The present church was built after a fire destroyed it in 1887. The Turkish name, "Sulu Manastır" was given because there is a holy spring in the substructure of the chapel.

Surp Hireşdagabedats (Church of the Archangels)

Location: Kamış Sok. Balat, on the Golden Horn F 1627 R 1730

This church stands on the site of a 13-14th century Byzantine church. The earlier sanctuary was dedicated to the "Taxiarchi" (chiefs) the archangels Michael and Gabriel who are referred to in historical religious literature as the chiefs of the celestial militia. The Armenian community took possesion of the church in 1629. There is a day of miracles on the second Friday of September when many with health problems attend and some are said to be cured. The church was restored in 1835.

Surp Kevork Lusavoriç (Church of St. George)

Location: Sakızcılar Sok. 3 Kemeraltı, Karaköy F 1361 R 1962

This is a farely new church near the site of the older one that was demolished in 1960 when the road was being widened.

It is a copy of the famous church in Echmiadzin, Armenia, that was built in the 7th century which is considered to be a masterpiece of Armenian architecture. The older church is said to have been of no special interest except that it had some unusual Tekfur tiles that can now be found in the crypt of the church where there is also a sacred spring. The older church was founded in 1360.

Surp Asdvadzazin (Church of the Blessed Virgin)
The Patriarchal Church

Location: Şarapnel Sok. No. 3, Kumkapı F 1641 R 1819

Surp Vorodman

The church complex consists of the cathedral with two side chapels of the Holy Cross and St. Vortovotz Vorodman. There is another chapel, that of St. Arthur which is between this cathedral and the Holy Cross chapel.

Location: Kumkapı on the grounds of the Patriarchate.

Surp Harutyun (Chapel of St. Arthur)

Location: Çakmak Taşı Sok. 35, Kumkapı F 1834 R 1855
Location: Sarayiçi Sok.7, Gedik Paşa F 1827 R 1950

Surp Tateos-Partogomeos
(Church of the Apostles Timothy and Bartholomew)

Location: Alboyacılar Sok. 57, Yenikapı F 1846 R 1969

Surp Hovhannes Avedaraniç

Location: Narlıkapı Cad. 150, Narlıkapı F 1807 R 1834

Surp Hagop (St. Jacob)

Location: Kırımlı Aziz Sok. 16, Ali Paşa, Altımermer F 1858 R 1892

Surp Nigogayos (St. Nicholas)

Location: Posta Yolu Cad. 159, Topkapı F 1626 R 1832

Surp Pirgiç (Christ the Savior)

Location: The Armenian Hospital,Yedikule F 1834 R 1966

Surp Asdvadzadzin (Church of the Blessed Virgin Mary)

Location: Ebuzziya Cad. 34, Bakırköy F 1831 R 1844

Surp Isdepanos (St. Stephen)

Location: İnci Çiçeği Sok.4, Yeşilköy F 1826 R 1984

Surp Yegya (St. Elias)

Location: Karayel Sok. 16, Eyüp F 18th c. R 1831

Surp Asdvadzadzin

Location: Kanun Sok. 5, Eyüp F 1785 R 1840

Surp Sarkıs Anıt Mezar

Location: Silivri Kapı Yolu 8, Balıklı F 1985

Surp Yerrortutyun (The Holy Trinity) Üçhorran

Surp Kevork

Location: Sahne Sok., Galatasaray F 1503 R 1810

Surp Yerrortutyun

Surp Harutyun (St. Arthur)
Location: Meşelik Sok. 34, Taksim F 1738   R 1895

Surp Vartant
Location: Şahadet Sok. 13, Feriköy F 1860   R 1903

Surp Asdvadzadzin
Location: İlhan Sok. 20, Beşiktaş F 1759   R 1838

Surp Asdvadzadzin
Location: Cibinlik Sok.5, Ortaköy F 1665   R 1835

Surp Haç (Church of the Holy Cross)
Location: Kırbaç Sok. 47, Kuruçeşme F 1798   R 1834

Surp Santuht
Location: Durmuş Dede Sok. 8, Rumelihisarı, F late 18th c. R 1856

Surp Yerits Mangants
Location: Aktar Apti Sok. 2/1 Boyacıköy, Emirgan F 1840 R 1984

Surp Asdvadzadzin
Location: Sahli Ağa Sok., Yeniköy F 1760   R 1834

Surp Hripsimyants
Location: Çayırbaşı Sok. 22, Büyükdere F 1848 R 1933

Surp Takavor
Location: Muvakithane Cad. 44, Kadıköy F 1720 R being restored

Surp Haç (The Holy Cross)
Location: Selamsız Kozanoğlu Sok. 3, Üsküdar F 1697 R 1727

Surp Garabed
Location: Yeni Mahalle Vasiyet Sok. 6, Bağlarbaşı - Üsküdar
F 1590   R 1838

Surp Kevork Lusavoriç (St. George)
Location: Çarşı Cad. 40, Kuzguncuk F 1835 R1967

Surp Yergodasan Arakelots (The Church of Twelve Apostles)
Location: Kurtbağrı Sok. 17, Kandilli F 1846 R 1962

Surp Nigogayos (St. Nicholas)
Location: Mehmet Yavuz Sok. 14, Beykoz F 1776 R 1946

Surp Nişan
Location: Soğanlık Sok. 6, Kartal F 1856

Surp Kevork Lusavoriç (St. George)
Location: Akgünlük Sok. 8, Kınalıada F 1855 R 1933

The early Christian psalms adhered to the music of the Jewish psalms. Often the early Christian churches were near a Jewish temple of worship and therefore had a tendency to imitate its musical form of worship. The ecclesiastical music of the Armenian church of the Middle Ages was highly developed and of outstanding beauty. It was comparable if not superior in quality only to that of the Byzantine Church. For anyone doing a study of the development of Eastern church music, one must take into account Armenian music and its influence in the development of Eastern chant.

Armenian Gregorian Church Choirs in Istanbul and the churches where they are found:

Kogtan   The Patriarchate in Kumkapı
Sahakyan   S.Kevork - Kocamustafapaşa
Varvaryan   S.Harutyun - Kumkapı
Zevartnots S.Hovhannes - Gedikpaşa
Karasun Manuk S.Asdvadzadzin - Bakırköy
Sahak Mesrob S.Istepanos - Vaniköy
Getronagan S.Kr. Lusavoriç - Karaköy
Asogik   S.Yerortutuin - Galatasaray
Lusavoriç   S.Harutyun - Taksim
Vartanants S.Vartanants - Feriköy
Narekatsi   S.Asdvadzadzin - Beşiktaş
Tarkmançats S.Asdvadzadzin - Ortaköy
Gomidas   S.Yerevman Khaç - Kuruçeşme
Sayat Nova S.Yeritz Mangants - Boyacıköy, Emirgan
Hiripsimyants S.Hiripsimyants - Büyükdere
S.Takavor   S.Takavor - Kadıköy
Miatsial   S.Khaç - Üsküdar
S.Garabet   S.Garabet - Bağlarbaşı, Üsküdar
S.Kr.Lusavoriç S.Kr.Lusavoriç - Kınalıada

Church of the Blessed
Virgin, Patriarchate

The Russian Orthodox Church

In the 10th century Vladimir, a Russian prince, was searching for a religion that would be suitable for his people. Being fond of women, he favoured the Islamic promise of carnal desires after death. But, also he learned that no wine was to be consumed by the members of Islam and he said, "Drinking is the joy of the Russians and we cannot exist without that pleasure". He found another excuse for not adopting Judaism. So he sent emissaries to Constantinople where they were so inspired by the resplendent liturgy at Hagia Sophia that they did not know whether they were in heaven or on earth, saying, "We only know that God dwells there among men. "Whereupon, in 988 Valdimir adopted the religion of Byzantium, was baptized in the Dnieper and also had his subjects baptized on the pain of death by the sword. So the story goes...

The Russians adopted Slavonic as their liturgical language. Monastic life was patterned after the religious life on Mount Athos. A native school of iconography developed together with church art and architecture, reaching its zenith between the 12-14th centuries. After the Mongols captured Kiev in 1240, the Metropolitan See was transferred to Moscow in 1328. Then with the fall of Constantinople to the Turks in 1453, Moscow became the most important center of Eastern Christianity, the "Third Rome", according to some historians of that period. During the reign of Peter the Great (1672-1725) the patriarchate was abolished and replaced by the Holy Synod whose members were nominated by the Tsar.

Monastic life, missionary activities, and the spiritual influence of the church flourished in the latter part of the 18th century and at the beginning of the 19th century Russian missions were established in Siberia, Alaska, and Japan. At the All Russian Council held during the 1917 Revolution, the patriarchate was restored.

But upon the death of the patriarch in 1925 the Soviet

government forbade the election of a new patriarch and the church was severely persecuted. In 1943 finally a new patriarch was elected. The church is governed by a Holy Synod under the presidency of the patriarch.

Until just after the Russian Revolution, there was a large Russian Orthodox community living in Istanbul, but there are only a few thousand left in Turkey today. This community has 3 churches in the Galata-Karaköy district but only one, St. Andrea's is active. The churches are a little difficult to locate since they are on the top floors of three separate buildings in the same neighbourhood. The buildings are owned by the Greek Orthodox Monastery of Mount Athos and were rented to the Russian Orthodox community as early as the 11th century to be used as lodgings by the Russian pilgrims on their way to and from Jerusalem. Today the buildings house the Russian pensioners who have settled in Turkey.

The church is under the jurisdiction of the Greek Orthodox Patriarchate. A priest from the Bulgarian Orthodox Church conducts services because the church does not have its own priest.

Church of St. Andrea (St. Andrew)

Location: Balyoz Sok. Galata, on the street parallel to Kemer Altı Cad. in the neighbourhood of the Tr. Orthodox Church.

Services are held every Sunday morning. on Dec. 13 there is always a special service for the feast day of St. Andrea. The church is on the top floor of the building. One of the interesting features of the church is that its church bells are inside the building, hanging from the top floor above the stairwell.

The Bulgarian Orthodox Church

The history of the Bulgarians, as of many other nations in Europe, seems to be like a game of table tennis involving politics, religion and geography. They settled in the country they now occupy and in the surrounding areas, fusing with the Slavs who were already there and adopted their language. Christianity was already established there but they did not embrace it until the 9th century when the Bulgarian tsar, Boris I (852) had been baptized by Byzantine priests and compelled his subjects to follow him. In the meantime in 862, Prince Rostislav of Moravia requested that the Byzantine Emperor, Michael III send him some missionaries who knew their Slavic language and could develop an alphabet that the people could use and read in their liturgy. So "The Apostles of the Slavs" namely Cyril (827-69) and Methodios (825-85) missionary brothers, were sent.

They were natives of Thessalonike and knew the vernacular language of that area. They invented an alphabet in which the language could be written and began to translate and write all the liturgy in "Cyrilic" named after its originator, Cyril. Some texts refer to it as Glagolitic. This language, Slavonic or Old Church Slavonic is used today in the church liturgy of some of the Orthodox churches and a few Catholic ones.

In 866 the disciples were driven out of Moravia and received by Boris who had them introduce the language into their liturgy. SS. Cyril and Methodios are recognized as saints by both the Orthodox and Roman Catholic churches. The latter commemorate their feast day on March 9 while the former commemorate St. Cyril's on Feb.14 and St. Methodios on May 11.

In 917 the Bulgarian church became a patriarchate during Tsar Simeo's reign (893-927). The patriarch established himself at Ochrida, Macedonia in 972. But the Byzantine emperor Basil II put an end to the independence of Bulgaria in 1020 and replaced the patriarchate with a Greco-Bulgar archbishop subject to Constantinople. The See was gradually being Hellenized. After the Bulgarians established an independent Bulgarian empire, again they recovered patriarchal rank and established the Patriarchate of Tirnovo which lasted from 1204-1393, as long as the Bulgarian Empire lasted. Under the Ottoman Empire both were suppressed and again Ochrida regained the patriarchate only to be abolished once more in 1767 and to come under the control of the Greek Orthodox Church.

With the approval of Sultan Abdulmecit in 1856, the Bulgarians living in Istanbul started a movement for a national Bulgarian church. Its religious independence was recognized by the imperial decree of Sultan Abdul Aziz in 1870. They were to have a national church governed by an Exarch, an ecclesiastical dignitary plus a number of bishops. The Bulgarian community was free to choose the Exarchate or to remain with the Greek Orthodox Patriarchate. The Exarchate was to serve as an intermediary between their church and the Turkish government. When the Exarch died in 1915 a new one was not appointed and since then there has only been a "locum tenens", a deputy acting for the Exarchate.

Church of St. Stephen

Location: On the Golden Horn, near the "Fener" pier

After the Bulgarians who had settled in Istanbul were allowed to have their own church, they erected a very original one in 1871 and named it after St. Stephen the first martyr of Christ. The patron saint's feast day is celebrated on Dec. 26.

The church was prefabricated in Vienna and sent in sections down the Danube to the Black Sea and finally to the shores of the Golden Horn where it was assembled and elegantly stands to this day. The surprising thing is that it is made of cast iron both internally and externally. It is Neo-Gothic in style and is certainly worth a visit. There is a small

Church of St. Stephen

group of Turkish citizens of Macedonian[1] origin who worship there and keep the church in the best condition.

The church is administered by a Board of Directors. The community has a cemetery in Feriköy and a community center in Şişli. Both of these places have chapels.

It is a tradition of the church to celebrate the Epiphany on Jan.6 when a cross is thrown into the Golden Horn or the Bosphorus and the youth dive in and try to retrieve it.

The church follows the Julian calendar. It has an active church choir that sings in Slavonic and on occasion sings at the various churches in the city. Services are held every Sunday at the chapel in Şişli and on special occasions at the church.

On Feb.1 the feast day of St. Triphon, the patron saint of gardeners is celebrated.

1   A people whose origins go back to the ancient country of Macedonia, a Balkan country that was divided among Bulgaria, Greece and Yugoslavia. It was once part of the Roman Empire. In the 5th century A.D. the Slavs began to invade and colonize Macedonia and it became in turn an independent kingdom, a part of the Bulgarian and later the Serbian empires. From the end of the 14th century until the Balkan War of 1912 it was under Turkish rule.

The Syrian Orthodox - Kadim Süryani

Among the first societies to accept Christianity were the Syrians during the first five years after the crucifixion of Christ and therefore have always used the phrase, ancient Syrians (Kadim Süryani). This group was made up of Aramis[1]. Their first church was founded in Antioch by the disciples SS. Peter and Thomas.

When Christianity became the official religion of both East and West Rome, the bishops serving the church of Antioch wanted their independence. There were various doctrinal controversies about the nature of Christ.

One such dispute was proposed by Arius, the patriarch of Alexandria, who received his theological education in Antioch. His views, Arianism[2], were to establish the unity and simplicity of the eternal God.

In order to put an end to the disputes within the various Christian groups over the nature of Christ, Constantine the Great called the first Church Council of Nicea (İznik) in 325. He really did not understand the dogmatic problem but saw that it might affect the hold he had on his vast empire. He wanted all Christians to be united in one belief, thus ensuring that the governing of his people be easier. 318 bishops attended, the majority being Greek. Arius and his followers were exiled as heretics and all their books were burned.

Arianism still carried on for more than a 100 years after the Nicean Council. Again in 451 the Council of Chalcedon was called to reach a decision and finally end all the arguments. This council taught that although Jesus Christ is God and man, he is but one Person, that is, one Person in two natures, one divine and one human. The bishops of the East were not invited, only the Byzantine and Roman bis-

---

1 A country or North Semitic kingdom extending from the western borders of Babylonia to the highlands of western Asia.
2 A heresy preached in about 323 A.D. by Arius a priest in Alexandria it denied the divinity of Christ, regarding him merely as a perfect man.

hops attended i.e those would act in accordance with the state's wishes. The church would then be officially declared the state church. In this way religion was becoming a tool of politics.

In the 5th century all the Christians of the Byzantine Empire were regarded as members of the official church. The patriarch of Antioch opposed this proposition and so the first seeds of the future schism were planted. The split occured in 518 A.D. when the Byzantine Church decided to be self-governing, to channel all state funds to itself and no longer to the patriarch of Antioch. This church was later named the Greek Orthodox Church.

Rites were taken into account also. During the first centuries certain cities such as Antioch, Jerusalem, Alexandria, Caesarea in Cappadocia, provided their communities with the ceremonies of worship. The Antiochene Rite was preserved by the Jacobites and was properly called the Syrian rite whose liturgical language was Aramaic, the language that Christ spoke.

The Ancient Syrian Church lost its center in Antioch and moved to other parts in the region like Aleppo, Harran, Rakka, and Kinnerşin as its patriarchal centers. Only after regaining possession of Antioch could the Ancient Syrian Church avoid persecution after the invasion of Islam. In 969 they settled in Malatya but the long arm of the state church reached them there too and they had to move to Diyarbakır. This was considered to be the permanent center where the patriarch resided.

When the Patriarch Ilyas III died during a trip to India in 1932 the Hums metropolitan Epherm I of Mosul was elected the patriarch. After this election the Ancient patriarchate settled in Damascus and is still there. In South India this creed is known as the Malabar Christians and their local head has the title of "Katholikos of the East". Another name given to this group is the Christians of St. Thomas.

Our interest in the Eastern rites services was drawn

when we were looking for a sacred spring in Samatya. By chance we saw a number of people coming out of a church. They were speaking Turkish and an Arabic dialect. We saw a priest and went over to talk to him. He was most friendly and told us that it was a Syrian Orthodox congregation and that they had just celebrated the Holy Day of St. Jonah (Yunus), the patron saint of the sea. It was the 11th of February and for the previous three days they had fasted. After the church service they had broken their fast with various foods and sweets.

We were given a communion "wafer" which was a large cookie with twelve squares imprinted on the surface representing the twelve apostles. This was the Dominican church of the Blessed Virgin. Since the congregation does not have a church of its own in that district, they have permission to use this Roman Catholic church. Their liturgical service at that time was in Aramaic. A notice in the church listed the various churches where services were held. This congregation has a monastery "Deyrulzafaran" in Mardin.

The Ancient Syrian Church of the Blessed Virgin - Süryani Kadim Meryem Ana Kilisesi

Location: Karakurum Sok. 22 Tarlabaşı, Beyoğlu

This is the only church that is owned by this creed and it is the residence of their Metropolite.

The other churches that are used for services are the Church of Mary of the Rosary in Bakırköy and the Church of Anastasia, in Gedikpaşa. The latter was owned by the Assumptionists. Then it was given to the Syrian Catholics before they moved to the Church of the Sacred Heart in Ayazpaşa.

The Turkish Orthodox Church

Church of the Panagia - The Blessed Virgin Mary

Location: Alipaşadeğirmenci Sok. 2, off Kemeraltı Cad., Karaköy. It is in the neighbourhood of the "Paket Postanesi"

This church is in a courtyard enclosed by a wall. The gate carries an emblem of a cross together with a star and crescent and is the symbol of the Turkish Orthodox Church.

The church was established by Papa Eftim who was the representative of the Greek Orthodox Archbishop of Keskin in the province of Ankara. He was considered a dissident of the Greek Orthodox Church because with the purpose of establishing this church he held a meeting in Kayseri attended by some archbishops and civic leaders. These events occurred during the Turkish War of Independence of 1919. Various political problems resulted within the Orthodox church, but eventually in 1924 the Central Board of the Pious Foundation, acting on behalf of the Religious Congregation of the Galata Region of Istanbul, invited Papa Eftim to take charge of the churches of St. Mary, St. Nicholas, and the Christ Church in Galata.

He accepted their invitation, was consecrated bishop in 1926, and was known by his congregation as Patriarch Efthemios I. Until his death he worked to establish a permanent Turkish Orthodox Church where religious services were held in Turkish.

This independent Patriarchate was administered by his son, Dr. Turgut Erenerol M.D. He had served as the Vice Patriarch of the church as Efthemios II since 1961 to 1991 when he passed away. His son Selçuk Erenerol is now heading the church.

The Greek Orthodox Churches in Istanbul

Historically what is known as the Orthodox church developed from the Church of East Rome or the Byzantine Empire. Its predominant influence was that of Greece. From the 9th century onwards there developed many different views between the Eastern and Western Sees which led to the gradual schism between the two groups. The development of the Greek Orthodox Church can be found under the section "Christianity and the division of the Eastern and Western Churches".

Of the large number of Greek churches in the city, two of them, St. Mary of the Mongols and St. George of the Cypresses (not the present building) remain from the Byzantine period. A number of churches were built much later. Most of the churches have precious chandeliers, candlesticks, icons and various religious objects. Since many of the churches were wooden structures, they were destroyed by earthquakes and city fires, and were rebuilt.

We have not been able to get the history of all the churches. The date given after the church's name designates its feast day. The Patriarchate is located at the Church of St. George on the Golden Horn at Fener where the Patriarch resides. He is the spiritual and Ecumenical Patriarch of all the Orthodox churches but his jurisdiction is limited to his flock in Turkey.

A short explanation of the word saint as used in Greek may be useful: "Ayios" means saint and comes from the old Greek. Its shortened and more popular form is "Ay". For the female saint "Ayia" is commonly used by the Turks. "Ayios" written in Latin letters became "Hagios" for the male saint and "Hagia" for the female saint. When "Panayia" is used, "Aya" is never put in front of the term. It is the favourite title of the Blessed Virgin Mary, "All Holy".

Ayios Yeorgios[1]:
The patriarchal Church of St. George (Apr.23)

Location: Sadrazam Ali Paşa Cad., Fener, The Golden Horn.

In 1591 when Murat III converted the Church of Pammakaristos to Fethiye Mosque the patriarchate was first installed at St. Dimitrius Kanabu at Balat and in 1601 to the present site. But the present church was not built until 1720. It has many relics and pilgrimages are made to this church. The "chrism", the sanctified oil of olive oil and balsam, usually used at baptism and other special religious functions, is blessed here.

Ayios Yeorgios

Location: Inside the walls along Vodina Cad., Fener

A Byzantine church built in 1132, burned down in 1730 and rebuilt. In 1913 it was rebuilt a second time. It is under the jurisdiction of the Jerusalem Metropolitan.

Panayia:
Church of the Blessed Virgin Mary (Aug.15 and the 1st of each month)

Location: Melekşah Sok. 2/2 Unkapanı

Ayios Nikolaos:
Church of St. Nicholas (Dec.6)

Location: Abdulaziz Paşa Cad. Ayakapı, the Golden Horn

A Byzantine structure that burned down in 1600 to be rebuilt in 1837. It is dedicated to sailors. Inside the church there is a glass model of a ship in their commemoration. There is also a small chapel in the church that has icons and paintings that are unfortunately in a state of decay.

Ayia Triada

---

1 Since many Greek churches have the same name, the English name is not repeated.

Ayios Taksiarhis:
Church of the Archangels (Nov.8)

Location: Ayan Cad., Balat

Panayia Balinu:

Location: Melikeme Atte Cad., Balat

The present church dates from 1730 but there is said to have been a church on the same spot with the same name as early as 1597. The caretaker told us that "Balinu" was the name of a fish that became the patron of that church.

Ayios Ioannis Vaptistis:
Church of St. John the Baptist (Jan.7 and also Nov.25 which is St. Catherine's Day)

Location: Not far from St. Stephen's Church on the Golden Horn.

This church dates from 1830 and is connected to the Metochion of Mount Sinai.

Ayia Triada:
Church of the Holy Trinity (51 days after Easter)

Location: Meşelik Sok. 11/1, Taksim, Beyoğlu.

Services are every Sunday at 09:00.

The capital of the Ottoman Empire attracted a great many Greeks who settled. Mainly in the districts of Fener, Beyoğlu and the islands. As the colony grew new churches were built, especially in the 19th century. This is one of them, built in 1882 and is the cathedral of the district. It is basilical in lay-out with three naves and has several Byzantine icons. It is one of the first churches with a dome.

Metamorphosis:
Church of the Transfiguration (Aug.6)

Location: Near the Greek cemetery in Şişli

Ayia Panayia

Ayios Apostoli:
Church of the Twelve Apostles (June 30)

Location: Evrenoszade Sok., Feriköy

Also known as the "Dodeka Apostoli" church and was built in 1868.

Ayios Dimitrius:
Church of St. Demetrius (Oct.26)

Location: Ateşböceği Sok.66, Kurtuluş

In 1527 there was a church of Ayios Haralambos on the grounds to which an addition was made in 1782 and it was renamed. The church is the cathedral of this district.

Ayios Athanasios:
Church of St. Athanasius (Jan.18)

Location: Omuzdaş Sok., Kurtuluş

Built in 1855.

Ayios Dimitrius:
Location: Sarmaşık Mahallesi, Edirnekapı

First built in 1780 and rebuilt after a fire in 1834.

Ayios Yeorgios:
Location: Kariye Yağnanesi Sok.1, Edirnekapı

This church was destroyed in a fire at an unknown date and rebuilt in 1836.

Ayios Nikolaos:
(feast days are Dec.6 and Sept.14)

Location: Sulukule Cad., Topkapı

Built in 1750, burned down in 1874 after which date it was restored.

Panayia:
Location: Haci Hamza Mektebi Sok. 65, Belgrad Kapı

Ayia Paraskevi: (July 26)

Location: Kazlıçeşme Mahallesi, Yedikule

Due to a tale of miracles that occured in the neighbourhood at the sacred spring, a small church was built on those grounds.

Ayios Kontantinos ke Eleni:
Church of SS. Constantine and Helen (May 21)

Location: Samatya Cad., Samatya

This church was built in 1805 and is one of the churches used by the Karamanlis[1] in their services. The building in its present state dates from 1955.

Ayios Nikolaos:

Location: Muallim Fevzi Sok., Samatya

St. Nicholas has been one of the most popular saints in Christendom being the patron saint of sailors, merchants and children. He was the Bishop of Myra (Demre) in Lycia which is located in southwestern Turkey. He is known as "Father Christmas" and Santa Claus. The latter name is derived from the Dutch dialect as "Sinte Klaas."

Analipsi:
Church of the Assumption (40 days after Easter)

Location: Akıncı Sok., Samatya

We were told that this church is over a thousand years old. There is an ayazma[2] on the grounds where special services are held on May 6 and Easter.

---

1 Christians belonging to the Greek Orthodox Church. For centuries they lived in Anatolia among the Turks and so did not speak Greek but Turkish. However, in their own schools they learned the Greek alphabet which came more easily to them than the Arabic one used by the Turks until a short time after World War I. Consequently they write in Turkish using Greek letters. Their church services are held in Turkish. When they immigrated to Istanbul from Anatolia they settled mainly in the districts of Kumkapı and Yedikule.

2 Ayazma, holy spring or sacred spring with special healing powers.

Ayios Yeorgios Kiparissas:
Church of St. George of the Cypresses (Apr.23)

Location: Samatya Cad., Samatya

This church was founded in the 9th. century and remained in the hands of the Greeks after the Turkish conquest. Fire destroyed it in 1782. The present building dates from 1832.

Ayios Minas: SS Karpos and Bapyios
Church of St. Menas (Nov.11)

Location: Samatya Cad., Samatya

The church was dedicated to Menas, a Patriarch of Constantinople. By royal decree of Sultan Mahmut II, the church was built in 1833 on the ruins of an old Byzantine church. Beneath the church is an interesting substructure, the Martyrium of SS. Karpos and Bapyios who were Christians from the 2nd or 3rd century. It is said to be the oldest surviving place of Christian worship in the city. The architecture of the martyrium is quite interesting. It is now unfortunately a place used to make stoves.

Panayia:
(Aug. 15 and on the Friday two weeks before Easter.)

Location: Şeker Hekimoğlu Ali Paşa Sok., Altı Mermer

Ayios Teodoros:
Church of St. Theodore (Friday before Easter)

Location: Namık Kemal Cad. on the grounds of a Greek. school, Yenikapı

Panayia:
Location: Samsa Sok.4, Kumkapı

Ayia Kiriyaki:
Church of St. Kiriyaki (July 7)

Location: Kadırgalimanı Cad. , Kumkapı

This is another church where the Karamanlis worship.

Panayia:

Nov. 21 and Sept. 24

Location: Emin Nevruz Sok. Galatasaray, Beyoğlu

Services every Sunday at 09:00

Ayios Konstantinos ke Eleni:

Location: Kalyoncukulluğu Cad.176, Beyoğlu

The building was started in 1856 and completed in 1861.

Ayios Dimitrius Kanabu: (Oct.26)

Location: Kırkambar Sok. 12, Balat

A Byzantine church known to have existed on the same spot and it served as the Patriarchal church for a few years. The present one dates from 1730.

Panayia Paramithias:

The Church of the Blessed Virgin, the Consoler

(July 2 and Friday 2 weeks after Easter)

Location: Mısmarcı Sok., Fener

This church is also called Valcherna (Valch-Saray) or the Palace of Wallachians. The Valchs claimed to be a Latin people (Rumen) from the south of the Danube. The church got its name because it was attached to their palace. It temporarily served as the patriarchal church from 1586-1596. At the entrance of the church there is a double eagle carved on a marble flagstone. It is the symbol of both the imperial Palaiologian dynasty and of the Greek Orthodox Patriarchate.

Panayia: (Aug. 15 and 31)

Location: Tandır Sok. , Eğri Kapı

Panayia ton Uranan:

Church of the Blessed Virgin Mary of the Dagger (Aug. 15)

Location: Ulubatlı Hasan Sok., Tekfursaray

Ayia Evangelistina:
Church of the Announciation (Mar.25)

Location: Hacıl Bey Sok. 6, Dolapdere

This church has an icon of the BVM which is said to have miraculous powers.

Ayia Paraskevi:

Location: Baçtar Sok. 2/1 ,Hasköy

Built in 1835. The church has a relic of Ayia Aryiro which is said to help cure ocular diseases.

Hristos:
Church of Christ

Location: Galata, Sakızcılar Sok. Kemeraltı Cad., next to Surp Kevork Lusavoriç

Ayios Nikolaos:

Location: Mumhane Cad., Galata

In the Byzantine period this church was called Ayios Andonius. The present building dates back to 1856 and is dedicated to sailors. Like its namesake in Cibali, it has a model ship hanging in the narthex. For the last 65 years it had been used by the Turkish Orthodox community.

Ayios Ioannis:

Location: Near Sakızlar Sok. and Kaval Sok., Galata

The church was built in 1843 by the Greeks from Chios. It is said to have been a Catholic church which had burned down a few times and the congregation did not have enough funds to restore it.

Panayia:

Location: Muallim Naci Cad., Beşiktaş

Ayios Fokas:
Church of St. Phokas (Sept.22)

Location: Muallim Naci Cad., Ortaköy

The church was built in 1856 and was dedicated to St. Phokas the Gardener who is stated to have been martyred in the Dioclation persecution.

Ayios Dimitrius:
Location: Kırkçeşme Sok., Kuruçeşme

The church was rebuilt in 1798 and it is not known when the original one was built. According to some sources a seminary and a Greek university were located here in 1804. In 1849 the seminary was transferred to Heybeliada and the university to Fener, neither one being in existence at the present.

Ayios Ioannis:
Location: Kuruçeşme Cad., Arnavutköy

The church was built in 1814 and was the summer church of the Patriarchate.

Ayios Taksiarhis:
Church of the Archangels (Nov.8)
Location: Kuruçeşme-Arnavutköy Yolu, Arnavutköy

Ayios Haralambos:
Church of St. Haralambos (Feb.10)
Location: İnşirah Sok., Bebek

The date of foundation is not known but it was connected to the Aynorozda Iviron monastery also in Bebek.

Ayia Evangelistina:
Church of the Annunciation (Mar.25)
Location: Boyacık Fırın Sok. 7, Boyacıköy

The name of the church commemorates the announcement of the Incarnation by the angel Gabriel to the Virgin and her miraculous conception of Christ, a dogma of the Christian Church.

Ayios Taksiarhis: (Nov.8)

Location: M. Sait Saraç Sok., İstinye

The prsent church was built in 1889 and has several icons and relics that were donated by Russian sailors.

Ayios Nikolaos:

Location: Sait Halim Paşa Cad., Yeniköy

The church burned down in 1772, rebuilt in 1812-14 and repairs were completed in 1839.

Panayia:

Location: Küçük Tepe Sok., Yeniköy

Ayios Yeorgios:

Location: Valide Çeşme Sok., Yeniköy

The church belongs to the Patriarchate of Jerusalem and was built in 1851.

Churches under the administration of the Metropolit of Terkos:
Ayia Paraskevi:

Location: On the Yeniköy-Tarabya Rd., Tarabya

Built in 1860, this church is the cathedral of the district.

Ayia Paraskevi:

Location: Danışmend Sok., Büyükdere

The church was built in 1831 in the shape of a ship. It has a sacred spring said to cure ocular diseases.

Ayios Ioannis:

Location: Yenimahalle, Sarıyer

Built in 1834.

Ayios Yeorgios:

Location: Ebuzzia Cad., Bakırköy

Built in 1832 and financed by gardeners.

Ayios Stefanos:

Church of St. Stephen (Jan.27)

Location: Between Mirasyedi and Kalendar Sok., Yeşilköy.

Built in 1845.

Churches under the administration of the Metropolit of the Prince Islands:

Ayios Dimitrius:

Location: Büyükada, Alacam Sok. Behind the Belediye Building.

Built in 1856, this is the cathedral of the four islands.

Ayios Nikolaos:

Location Heybeliada, İmralı Aralığı Sok.

Built in 1857

Panayia Pammakaristos:

The Chapel of the Blessed Virgin Mary, the Joyous Mother of Christ.

Location: It is on the grounds of what used to be the Turkish navy school.

This small chapel is attributed to Maria Komnena in the 14th century. It is a quatrefoil chapel, having a central dome resting on four semi-domes along the axes, but due to rebuildings little of its original plan exists today. The only other church built on this plan is St. Mary of the Mongols. Nearby is the tomb of Sir Edward Burton, ambassador of Queen Elizabeth I to the Sublime Porte. In 1596 the ambassador accompanied Mehmet II on his campaign to Hungary but falling ill on his return, came to the island to rest. He died there in 1596.

Panayia: (Sept.8)

Location: Kınalı Ada, Beşiroğlu Sok.

Ayios Ioannis:

Location: Burgazada, Takımağa Meydanı

The first Byzantine structure was built in 867 A.D. The present building of 1896 was built on the cave of St. Methodios.

Monasteries with churches:

Panayia: (one week after Easter on a Friday)

Location: Balıklı Çırpıcı Cad., Silivrikapı

The church connected to the monastery is called the "Balıklı Kilise", the Church of the Fish, because of a legend connected to the spring that is found in the chapel of the church. The spring is said to have had fish which were brown on one side. Supposedly this colouring was inherited from their ancestors, the fish that had jumped from a monk's frying pan when the news came that the city was taken by the Turks.

Several Byzantine emperors built churches here, but the present one dates back only to 1833. The Greek Orthodox still frequent the holy spring which is believed to perform miraculous cures. Of special interest is the inner courtyard which is paved with tombstones in Turkish using the Greek alphabet (the Karamanlı script.)

Connected to the monastery are a home for the elderly and a hospital. There are two separate churches; Ayia Anagin (July.1 and Nov.1) and Ayios Haralambos (Feb.10). Many religious dignitaries are buried on the grounds.

Metamorphosis:
Church of the Transfiguration (Aug.6)

Location: Büyükada

This church commemorates the appearance of the Lord in glory during his earthly life.

Ayios Nikolaos:
Location: Büyükada, by the horse-carriage station

This Byzantine church was rebuilt in 1868.

Ayios Yeorgios:
(Apr. 23 and Sept. 24)

Location: Büyükada

It is said to have been built in 857 A.D. and rebuilt in 1844 as a seminary which was closed in 1970.

Metamorphosis:
Location: Heybeliada

This church commemorates the appearance of the Lord in glory during his early life.

Ayios Yeorgios:
Location: Heybeliada, on the hill above the Military School.

The present building is from 1862 with some restorations that were carried out in 1945

Monasteries belonging to the Patriarchate of Jerusalem:
Ayios Yeorgios on Burgazada,
Location: Gönüllü Cad. No. 76 F 1897

Churches under the administration of the Metropolit of Kadıköy:

Aya Efemia:
Church of St. Euphemia (July 11 and Sept.16)
Location: Corner of Mühürdar Cad. Yasa Cad., Kadıköy.

Dedicated to the virgin and martyr saint of the 4th century. It was a Byzantine church which fell into ruins in time. In 1694 the Kadıköy Metropolit got permission to renovate it with funds donated by Russia.

Ayia Triada:
(51 days before Easter)
Location: Between Hacı Şükrü Sok. and Bahariye Cad. Moda Built in 1902.

Ayios Yeorgios:
Location: Yeldeğirmen, Kadıköy

It was built as a school in 1895 and another building was added in 1918. After further repairs the buildings were converted to a church in 1927.

Ayios Ioannis Hrisostomos:
Church of St. John Chrysostom (Jan.27)
Location: Kalamış, Kadıköy

Its date of foundation is unknown but it is said to have been built on a Byzantine cemetery. The church was dedicated to St. Chrysostom who was a Bishop of Constantinople and a "Doctor of the Church". He was ordained in 386 A.D. and being a very able preacher gained the name of Chrysostom, "golden mouthed."

Prophitis Ilias:
Church of the Prophet Elijah (July 20)
Location: Bağlarbaşı, Üsküdar

Dedicated to one of the Old Testament prophets of the 9th century B.C.

Ayios Panteleemon:
Church of St. Pantaleon (July 27)
Location: İcadiye Cad. 80, Kuzguncuk
The present church was built in 1896. It was dedicated to this saint who was a martyr of the Diocletian Persecution. He was one of the patron saints of physicians.

Ayios Yeorgios:
Location: Kuzguncuk
Built on the foundation of a 6th century church.

Ayios Yeorgios:
Location: Kuleli Cad., Çengelköy
Built in 1830 on a Byzantine monastery.

Metamorphosis:
Location: Kandilli

Panayia:
Location: Göksuyu

Ayios Konstantinos:
Church of St. Constantine (May 21)
Location: Çağtay Sok., Paşabahçe
This church was completed in 1894. In the Eastern Church St. Constantine has been named the "Thirteenth Apostle". He was the son of St. Helen.

Ayia Paraskevi:
Location: Panayır Sok., Beykoz
The church was built in 1852 and was illuminated with candles until 1937. After that date a benefactor had it electrified. From 1940-43 it was used as a military warehouse, then from 1943-45 as a warehouse of the Tekel Office. In 1945 it was turned over to the church's Board of Directors.

The Anglican Churches

Chapel of St. Helena

Location: On the grounds of the British Consulate in Galatasaray.

The chapel has existed since the time of Queen Eliza-beth I (1533-1603) when she sent an ambassador to the Sub-lime Porte along with a priest who was connected to the dip-lomatic mission in Istanbul. The present chapel was built in the mid-19th century because the original wooden chapel and the embassy burnt down as a result of Istanbul's many fires. It was built as a traditional English church. There are interesting marble plaques in the church.

One of the plaques is "This chapel was erected in 1882 from the plans of W.L.Lynn Esq. of Belfast under the auspi-ces of His Excellency the Earl of Dufferin, her Brittanic Majesty's Ambassador to the Sublime Porte". There is a flagstone that is dedicated to The Rev. Thomas King Pastor of Constantinople, 1618.

The church was established as an Anglican (Episcopali-an) church. It is in communion with and recognizes the le-adership of the See of Canterbury. St. Helena's is under the jurisdiction of the Bishop of Gibraltar. In the 1920's the Greek Patriarchate recognized the priests here as members of the Orthodox Union of Churches. The church has many activities that contribute to the welfare of the Turkish com-munity.

Sunday morning prayer is at 09:30. The Eucharist service is at 10:00 and Sunday school is held at 10:00 in the vestry.

The Crimean Memorial Church:

Location: At the back of the Swedish Consulate on İstiklal Cad. When walking down İstiklal Cad. towards Tünel take the first left after the consulate and walk down to the end of the street. Take a left on Şahkulu Bostanı Sok. At the end of this street, take a right and the church can be seen.

This impressive Neo-Gothic church was built in commemoration of the British soldiers who died in the Crimean War of 1854-56, to serve the British community living in the Pera section and the Anglican traders in the city. The cornerstone was laid in 1858 by Lord Stratford de Radcliffe who served as the British ambassador for 40 years. The land on which the church stands was donated by Sultan Abdul Mecit to the British government. The church was built by a famous British architect, George Edmund Street.

The Bishop of Gibraltar consecrated the church in 1868. After being abandoned the building was neglected and deconsecrated in 1976. Present plans are being carried out by the Anglican and British community to restore the church and preserve the momentoes found there.

The Church of the All Saints:

Location: Yusuf Kemal Sok. Moda, Kadıköy

It was established in the 1830's for the community that lived on the Asiatic side of Istanbul. The church is not too active at present but once every two weeks on Wednesday mornings at 11:00 there is a service for the English speaking community.

The Crimean
Memorial
Church

The Protestants and Their Churches

The Armenian Protestants

In 1831 William Goodell arrived in Istanbul as the first Protestant missionary, representing the American Board of Commissioners for Foreign Missions. H.G.O. Dwight joined him the following year and the Mission of the American Board to the Armenians was founded. Their first mission was in Ortaköy on the Bosphorus where already an Armenian, John Den Sahakian came to join them and acted as an interpreter of the Protestant message to the Armenian population in Istanbul.

He was appointed in 1834 as the general superintendant of the mission high school then recently opened in Pera. This school proved to be short lived. Conservative elements in the community looked upon them with suspicion and a priest was sent by the patriarchate to inspect the school. Then the students' parents were summoned to withdraw their sons from the mission school.

Schools in Hasköy, Ortaköy and Samatya were opened just to be closed a few years later. In 1840 a mission high school was reopened in Bebek under the supervision of Cyrus Hamlin.

The first Armenian Evangelical Church in Istanbul was established in 1846 and services were held in a chapel that was in Dwight's rented house that was opposite the grounds of the British Embassy.

In 1847 the first imperial decree was issued recognizing the Protestants of the country as a separate community and granting them freedom of conscience and worship.

The following churches hold Sunday morning services to very small congregations.

Ermeni Protestant Kilisesi:
Balipaşa Yokuşu 27, Kumkapı

Surp Ohannes Kilisesi:
Location: Sarayiçi Sok. 7/A, Gedikpaşa

Surp Ohannes Ermeni Protestant Kilisesi:
Location: Emin Camii Sok., (next to the German Protestant Church) Aynalıçeşme, Tarlabaşı.

The Dutch Chapel - The Union Church of Istanbul

Location: Postacılar Sok., Beyoğlu, situated in the Back of the Consulate of the Netherlands.

This one of the oldest Protestant churches in Istanbul for the English - speaking communities. The legations of Britain, Germany, Sweden and the Netherlands took on the responsibility of protecting the religious affairs of the Protestants who were both members and non-members of their communities and whose religious and ethnic rights were respected by the Ottoman government and as they are also today.

The grounds of the present Dutch Consulate were bought and established as an embassy in 1709. For years the ministers of the Dutch Reformed Church served in the embassy's chapel. American missionaries began their work in Istanbul in 1831. The Scottish mission was established in 1857. During this period there were many English - speaking foreigners working in Istanbul who worshipped in this Chapel.

For a while the church had mainly a British congregation. The American Protestants met separately. The two
congregations later united to establish "The Evangical Union of Pera" and in the 1960's the church was renamed "The
Union Church of Istanbul".

Its constitution of 1888 states that the "church shall not
belong to any distinctive denominations" and the church ta-
kes part in many ecumenical events with other religious groups in the city. In November 1982 it celebrated its 125th anniversary. The church choir has given concerts of major cho-
ral works. It also has a special "Bell Choir" that performs at
Christmas and on other occasions. From its beginning the
government of Netherlands has been most helpful in many
ways in allowing the use of the chapel on the grounds of
their consulate.

Services are held every Sunday at 09:30 and 11:00 in the
morning.

The German Protestant Church

One of the first Protestant ministers to the Ottoman
Empire was Stephan Gerlach who arrived in 1571. He was
followed by S. Schweigger in 1578 as the pastor of the German legation and continued the work started by gerlach in
the ambassador's home. For a period the establishment of
an independent Protestant parish was impossible. During a
meeting with the Protestant princes in Offenbach in 1742,
the Swedish representative supported a plan to establish a
Protestant church in Istanbul. With the permission of the
"Sublime Porte" the foundation of a chapel on the grounds
of the Swedish embassy grounds was consecrated in 1757
and services were held in German. In 1818 the Swedish
Embassy burned down along with the chapel and for about
50 years there was no church. But the religious needs of the
Protestant Germans were met in the Prussian Embassy. In
1843 the German Protestants met to establish a permanent
German Protestant church. The German Society built a

school on Ayanlıçeşme Emin Sok., Tepebaşı and it was opened in 1857. Finally the time came to build a church and it was decided to build it over the school, thereby using the same building. The church was consecrated in 1861.

The organ in the church dates back to 1884 when it arrived from Potsdam, Germany. Up to 1918 organ recitals were frequently held. The outward appearance of the church as we see it today dates back to its extensive renovation in 1911.

Services are held every Sunday at 10:30.

Church of the Seventh Day Adventists
Location: Saray Arkası Sok. 14, Ayazpaşa, Taksim

The first congregation was established in 1899. As the years went by the membership declined. At present there is a small group that worships at their church which was built in 1958.

Services are held Saturdays at 10:00 in Turkish and English.

The Swedish Protestant Church
Location: Saraskerci Çıkmazı Sok. 11, İstiklal Cad. Tünel, Beyoğlu

It is on the grounds of the Swedish consulate and can be reached by following the road that goes down to the Crimean Memorial Church. This small church, the Svenska Kyrka, was built in 1758 with the permission of the Swedish King Carl XII when he was visiting the city. When the Swedish Embassy burned down in 1818, the chapel was destroyed, also. Rebuilding it was not possible until 1858 and then it was used by the Greek Protestants.

In 1985 this small church was renovated and is presently being used by various Protestant groups . Services are on Sundays at 10:30 in Turkish.

The Syrian Protestants

1852 some of the Ancient Syrian Orthodox Christians converted to Protestantism. A small group of them exist in Istanbul and since they do not have a church of their own, worship in the various Protestant churches of the city. In spite of their religious divisions, all the Syrian and Chaldean groups have a brotherly relationship because their differences have never made them forget their common "Eastern" background.

The Emmanuel Chapel
The Near East Mission Bldg.

Rıza Paşa Yokuşu Fincancılar, Sirkeci

There is no date as to the building of the chapel, only that it must have been built at the same time as the first building, the Bible House, was built in 1884. It is a Turkish speaking Protestant community attended by a broad range of members. Services are carried out by lay-leaders on Sundays.

References

Byzantium

Bizans Devleti Tarihi-George Ostrogorsky-Türk Tarihi Kurumu

Bizans Tarihi-Auguste Bailly-Tercüman Gazette

Byzantine Churches in Constantinople-Van Milligen-London 1899

Byzantine World- J.M. Hussey-Harper and Brothers-New York 1961

Byzantine World-M. Bains

Byzantine Civilization-Sir Stephen Runciman

Byzantine Empire-C. Oman-London 1892

Byzantine Civilization-H.W. Haussing-Thames and Hudson

Byzantine and Russian Painting-Kostas Papaioannou-Funk and Wagnalls New
    York 1965

Byzantine Empire-The National Geographic Dec. 1983

Byzantium and Istanbul, the city as it stands today-Robert Ligi-Oxford Press 1956
    Byzantium, the City of New Rome- Cyril Mango-London 1980

Byzantium-Tamara Talbot Rice-Stellar Press 1969

Byzantium, (The last centuries of), 1261-1453 - D.Hicks and R.Hart Davis, Lon-
    don

Byzantium, Constantinople, Istanbul-Doğan Gümüş-Do-Gü Yayınlar

Calendars

Annuaire Ecclesiastique et Calendrier Liturgique

Vicariat Apostolique d'Istanbul 1988

Türkiye Ermeni Patrikliği Kilise Takvimi 1988-89

Christianity

Christ, the Teaching of-Lawler and Wuerl 2nd ed.-1983

Chirstianity, (The Rise of)-W.H.C. Frend-Darton-Longman and Todd 1984

Christianity- R.H. Bainton-American Heritage- New York 1985

Christendom, Eastern-Nicolas Zernov-Weidenfeld and Nicolson- London 1961.

Hıristiyan Türkler-Baykurt Camii-Istanbul 1932

Churches

The Early Churches of Constantinople- T.Mathew-Penn. State Univ. Press

The Dissident Eastern Churches-D. Attwater- Bruce Pub. Co. Millwaukee Wisc.
1937

The Catholic Eastern Churches-D. Attwater

The Separated Eastern Churches-Pere R.Janin-Herder Book Co.St. Louis Mo.
1933

Eastern Orthodox Churches-E. Benz-Doubleday

Christian Churches, Atlas of-edited by H. Chadwick and G. Evans MacMillan 1987

The Union Church of Istanbul, (A History of)- A. Edmonds-Ist. 1986

La Chiesa di S.Pietro in Galata-Palazzo e Raineri-Hartı Basıımevi 1943

Constantinople

Constantinople, (The City of), 324-1453-John E.N. Hearsey

Constantinople- Goble and Van Millingen 1913

Constantinople, (A Touristic Guide)-E.Mamboury-1st ed.

Constantinople, Ancient-Grosvenor-Lowand Marston-London 1895

Dictionaries

The Penguin Dictionary of Religions-edited by J.R. Hinnells 1984

The Penguin Dictionary of Saints-edited by D.Attwater 1965

The Modern Catholic Dictionary-J.Hardon-Doubleday and Co. 1980

The Oxford Dictionary of the Christian Church -revised and edited by Cross and
Livingstone 1974.

Encyclopedias

The New Catholic Encyclopedia-McGraw Hill 1967.

Encyclopedia Britannica 1961

Encyclopedia International 1971

Guide Books

Handbook for Travellers-J. Murray

Blue Guide-John Freely

Strolling Through Istanbul-Sumner-Boyd and Freely-Redhouse Yayınevi 83

Hagia Sophia-Nurettin Can Gülekli-Tr. Press, Broadcasting and Tourist Dept.

History

History of Civilization-Brinton, Christopher and Wolff-Prentice Hall 57

The Herbert History of Art and Architecture, Early Christian and Byzantine-Irmgard Hutter-Herbert Press 1988

A History of Religion, East and West-Trevor Ling-MacMillan 1985.

At the Threshold of Felicity-Ottoman-Dutch Relations 1726-1744.

History of Syri-P.Hitti-MacMillan 1951

The Concise Oxford History of Music-G.Abraham-Oxford Univ. Press 1979

The Ottoman Centuries-Lord Kinros-Morrow Quill Paperbacks N.Y. 1977

New Oxford History of Music part II, ed.by Don Anselm Hughes 1954.

Turkey Today-Grace Ellison-Mayflower Press, Plymouth

Eastern Anatolia and the Urartians- Afif Erzen - Türk Tarih Kurumu Basimevi 1984.

Turkey in Europe-Odysseus Eliot-Edward Arnold, London 1900

The Crusades by Harold Lamb 1956

History of the Ottoman Empire and Modern Turkey Vol.I-S.Shaw Cambridge Univ. Press, 1976.

Roma Imparatorluğunun Gerileyişi ve Çöküşü - Edward Gibbo-translated to Turkish by Asım Baltacıgil.

Istanbul Tarihi, 17nci asırda Istanbul - E. Çelebi Kömürciyan-Eren Yayıncılık 2. baskı 1988

Polonyalı Simeon'un Seyahatnamesi 1608-1619-Hrand D. Andreasyan-Baha Matbaası 1964.

Deutschsprachige Katolik Gemisind in der Türkei 1954-1979- H.Wilschowit.

Istanbul

Istanbul-W.A. Verlag-Munich

Istanbul-Uğur Ayyıldız

Istanbul 18. asırda- P.G. Inciyan-Baha Matbaası 1976

Istanbul and Environs-Hachette 1961

Istanbul, Imperial- Jane Taylor-Weidenfeld and Nicolson-London 1989

Istanbul Arkeoloji Müzeleri, Yunan, Roman, Bizans-Milli Eğitim Basimevi 66

Istanbul, A Traveller's Companion-L.Kelly, Constanble and Co. London 1989

Religion

The Modern Readers Guide to Religions- H. Watts-Barnes and Noble, 1964

A Handbook of Living Religions- J.R. Hinnelis- Viking 1984.

World's Religions, Illus. History of Ed. G.Parrinder,-Newness 1983.

Süryani

Süryani Türklerinin Siyasi ve İçtimai Tarihi- M. Sertoğlu-Baha Maatbasi 74

Süryani Olayı-Güneş Gaz. 27 Mart 1988

Süryaniler, Kadim Süryaniler ve Türkiyede'ki Durumlar-Kemal Özbay

Armenians

Kudüs Ermeni Patrikhanesi-Yavuz Ercan-Tr. Tarihi Kurumu 1988

The Armenians-David Marshall Lang-Union Hyman Ltd. London 1981

Impression of Turkey- W.M. Ramsay-Hodder and Stoughton, London 1987

The Armenian Awakening-Leon Arpee, Univ. of Chicago Press 1909

On Horseback Through Asia Minor-F.Burnaby- Hippocrene Books, N.Y. 1985

My Life and Times-Cyrus Hamlin-Pilgrim Press, Boston 1893

Armenian Churches of Istanbul by Pars Tuğlacı İst. 1991

Miscellaneous

Journal of a Soul-trans. by D.White-McGraw Hill 1964.

Turing Bulletin-Oct.1983 no. 70/349

Y A P I   K R E D İ   Y A Y I N L A R I   ▪   S A N A T

Yazılar Alberto Giacometti

İslam Sanatının Oluşumu Oleg Grabar

Duhuldeki Deney Mustafa Irgat

Zaman İçinde Müzik Evin İlyasoğlu

Cemal Reşit Rey haz. Evin İlyasoğlu

Necil Kâzım Akses haz. Evin ilyasoğlu

Deneysel Sinemacı Kimliğiyle Andy Warhol Sabri Kaliç

İstanbul'da Osmanlı Dönemi Rum Kiliseleri M. Zafer Karaca

Sveti Stefan Bulgar Kilisesi Hasan Kuruyazıcı - Mete Tapan

Albastı Defterleri Fikret Mualla

Churches In Istanbul Edith Oyhon - Bente Etingü

Resmin Gölgesi Şiire Düştü haz. M. Kayahan Özgül

Abdullah Frères (Tr.) haz. Engin Özendes

Abdullah Frères (İng.) haz. Engin Özendes

Kapadokya Kaya Kiliselerinde Üç Gün Yorgo Seferis

Şenlikname Düzeni Sezer Tansuğ

Yazı ve Mimari Hüseyin İlter Taşkıran

Ben, Sali Salih Turan

Balta/zar İzzet Yasar

İstanbul Resim Heykel Müzesi Kataloğu

http://www.shop.superonline.com/yky